RAINHA
PRESS

ISBNs:	eBook	979-8-9931072-8-8
	Paperback	979-8-9931072-7-1
	Hardcover	979-8-9931072-9-5

www.ajbishopandrews.com

Rich
Like Her

**FOUR WOMEN REDEFINING
SUCCESS, RECLAIMING
POWER, AND NAVIGATING
WEALTH ON THEIR
OWN TERMS**

AJ BISHOP-ANDREWS

RAINHA
PRESS

Contents

Dedication

To my mother, Antonieta, a true FEROZ woman, who stepped into the fire of uncertainty with a courage that still teaches me today. With only a third-grade education, she left Brazil for the United States, determined to build a better future for her young daughter—my oldest sister. FEROZ means fierce— not in force but in faith. It's the clarity to see your path and the conviction to walk it, even when the way forward is unknown.

To my sisters, Estella and Andrea, and my nieces, Iris and Jaylynn, for your unwavering love and for standing with me in both my wildest dreams and my lowest valleys.

To my husband, Tim—the love of my life and my rock. My greatest successes and deepest joys have been possible because of you. This book exists because of your encouragement and our shared vision for what's possible for women and wealth. I also honor your mother, Mary Ellen, whose strength in raising four children after divorce shaped the man you are and reminds me daily of the resilience and power women carry.

To my stepsons, Tyler, Joshua, and Noah. Thank you for teaching me the layered, complicated, and beautiful dynamics of being a stepmother. Through you, I have learned that family is not only what you are born into but also what you choose and grow with courage, patience, and love.

To the women who shaped me—and the ones I've yet to meet: May you hold two truths at once—that success and influence are your birthright, and that you have the power to shape them into a legacy wholly your own.

Disclaimer & Privacy Note

The women in this book are fictional composites, inspired by themes and truths the author has witnessed in over two decades of wealth management. Names and identifying details have been changed to respect privacy. This book is intended for reflection and education, not as financial, legal, or accounting advice.

Some chapters reference online resources or communities. If you choose to engage, any personal information you share will be collected, only with your consent, and used solely for delivering content and never sold. For full details, visit *www.ajbishopandrews.com.*

Before We Begin

THERE'S A VERSION OF YOU WHO'S DONE EVERYTHING "RIGHT," and yet something still feels... off. Not broken. Not lost. Just standing at a crossroads you never planned for—looking back at everything you've built and quietly wondering if the life you chased still fits.

You've built a beautiful life. You've been responsible. Strategic. Grateful. Adaptive. You did everything they said would lead to fulfillment. And still, there's that quiet voice you try to hush—the one that asks, *Is this it?*

Maybe you're stepping out of a role that once defined you—a career, a marriage, a partnership, or a version of yourself. Maybe something ended. Or maybe nothing ended at all, except the illusion that checking every box would ever feel like enough.

You haven't failed. You've simply outgrown the invisible rulebook of success, power, and wealth—the one that keeps women running faster, aiming higher, and pushing harder, only to wonder why it never feels satisfying.

Rich Like Her isn't about burning it all down—or chasing what someone else has. It's about sovereignty: shaping success, power, and wealth on your own terms. The kind no one can give you and no one can take away. The kind that begins not with doing more, but with finally becoming more of yourself than you ever thought possible.

And here's the truth no one says out loud: you don't have to start over. You can begin again—from here, exactly where you stand. You can take what you've built, what you've survived, what you've learned—and shape it into a life that finally feels like yours.

This book is a remembering. A reclamation. A mirror.

Through the stories of four women, you'll see yourself reflected—not in their circumstances but in their questions. In their courage to look beneath the surface. In their willingness to trace the patterns, name the truth, and choose what comes next.

Because this isn't just a fictional story. It's a story that women have lived—again and again—for generations.

For more than twenty years, I've helped women navigate money, power, and transition—not just as a wealth strategist, but as a guide in designing lives that feel as rich on the inside as they look on the outside.

That longing is what called me to write this book.

By 2035, women will control the majority of the world's wealth. Yet most still don't feel confident making financial decisions.

This is our inflection point.

What comes next isn't another lesson in financial literacy or empowerment—because neither has created the shift we truly need. It's a new beginning. The moment you stop performing wealth, power, and success—and start defining them on your terms.

Not because the women in these pages are you, but because you'll recognize yourself in the pause between who you've been and who you're becoming. That's where the real journey starts. That's where *Rich Like Her* begins.

If you've been waiting for permission to want more—something true, something alive, something that feels like what I call Whole Woman Wealth™—this is it.

You can have it all, once you decide what *all* really means.

You've built the life they told you to want. Now it's time to claim the one you were meant to live—rich, not as they defined it, but as only you can.

No Chair Left at the Table

the cost of chasing power in
rooms that were never yours

FROM THE OUTSIDE, AVA LOOKED LIKE THE WOMAN EVERY BUSI-
ness magazine profiled—polished, unshakable, in control. Inside,
she was counting down the moment she could take off her shoes
and breathe.

One scan of the room, and she saw them: four men in nearly
identical navy suits, whiskey glasses half-empty, the table already
full. David, one of the firm's senior leaders, was in her seat. No
RSVP, no hesitation. He had just slid into her spot.

Her calendar mirrored her life: overcrowded, overbooked, so
tangled with overlaps she couldn't keep track anymore. Proof
that the system she'd mastered was quietly mastering her.

Her 7:30 p.m. reservation—the deal she couldn't afford to
miss—was already in motion without her. And she'd skipped
Emma's school play for it. Her sister's disappointed text still
sat unanswered on her phone, a reminder that her work always
seemed to cost someone else something.

She'd built the strategy—every detail—yet there was no chair
at the table. Maybe there never was for women like her. Tyler and
Mark were the ones "building confidence," while the actual business decisions lived in late-night drinks and quiet text threads
that she was never part of. It was the same equation everywhere:

what she gave up at home and what she lost at work were just two sides of the same system designed to keep women like her out.

As she walked up, Tom laughed and gripped David's shoulder like they'd been old golf buddies for years. The circle was tight, laughter low, every tilt of their heads saying what she already knew: she was late to a game she hadn't even been told was on.

Heat shot through her chest. She forced her face into neutrality.

The maître d' arrived with a chair, wedging it between Tom and David like she was an afterthought. Or worse, an inconvenience.

Ava sat, straightened her napkin, and waited for the shift that never came. Tom's eyes never left David.

"As I was saying," Tom leaned forward, "your quarterly analysis hit the mark."

David smiled, looping her in. "Ava's been instrumental in shaping our strategic approach. You'd be surprised how much she's contributed."

Surprised. The word landed wrong. He meant it as inclusion, maybe even praise, but felt like dismissal.

Ava smiled politely and leaned in. "Tom, the strategy we built was designed specifically around your market pressures. That's why it's working."

Tom didn't glance her way. His gaze stayed locked on David, erasing her with the ease of someone who'd done it before and gotten away with it.

Ava tapped a slow rhythm against her water glass, the sound dulled by linen. Inside, tension coiled tight. By now, she'd lost count of how many times she'd been erased from the very table she set.

A pause followed, the kind that begged for acknowledgment. None came. Tom's gaze never wavered from David, and the table slipped back into its rhythm without her, as if she hadn't spoken at all.

She kept her smile, the one she'd perfected for client events and impossible rooms. The conversation rolled on without her, the men leaning in over tumblers, swapping sports stats like she wasn't sitting at the same table.

I'm here, and I'm invisible anyway.

Ava excused herself before the salmon had even cooled, murmuring something about a call she needed to return. The truth was, she couldn't take one more minute of nodding at conversations she wasn't part of.

She thought of Emma on stage tonight, scanning the crowd for a face that never showed.

The mahogany door swung shut behind her, muting the clink of ice and low rumble of voices. She leaned back against the cool marble, trying to slow her breathing.

She adjusted. Practiced the smile. It would hold long enough to get her through the meal.

She was still adjusting her expression when a door opened. Sophia Duval stepped out of a stall in effortless grace, the kind of presence that lit up a bathroom before she even spoke. Black McQueen pantsuit, tailored so sharp it looked like armor. Blonde hair smooth, not a strand out of place. Lipstick red, the kind Ava always bought but never wore without second-guessing.

She stopped mid-stride. "Ava!" Surprise flickered warm across her face. "Didn't expect to see you here tonight."

Ava's shoulders tightened before she could stop them. She smoothed it away, summoning her event smile. "Sophia. I didn't realize you were here."

"Client brought me as their plus-one," Sophia said, rinsing her hands. She reached for a folded cloth towel from the silver tray, meeting Ava's eyes in the mirror as she dried them. "We're at the table by the window, timing how long these guys can congratulate each other without letting a woman get a word in. Twenty-eight minutes so far."

Her mouth curved, but the humor didn't quite reach her eyes.

Ava huffed out a small laugh, the sound more air than amusement.

"Wow, it's been a minute. I've missed seeing you," Sophia said. "Remember those stand-up meetings that dragged on forever? We swore the only way through was cocktails after."

The memory softened something in Ava's chest, a reminder of when it felt like she wasn't the only one in the grind. But even as she smiled, the unspoken comparison landed. Three years gone, and Sophia had vaulted to VP at her new firm. No endless politics. No golden children blocking the ladder.

"You seem good," Ava said. "New firm treating you well?"

"Busy, but in a way that doesn't make me want to fake food poisoning to get a day off," Sophia said with a dry smile. "What about you? Still running point on everything?"

Ava gave the practiced answer. "You know me."

Keep moving, stay moving. That was the rule.

Sophia studied her for a beat, like she heard more in Ava's words than Ava meant to give away. "Can I ask you something? No filters?"

Ava searched Sophia's face, waiting for the competition she'd learned to anticipate. Instead, there was only curiosity. "Sure."

"When's the last time you did something because you wanted to," Sophia asked, "and not because it would look good on LinkedIn?"

Ava blinked, caught between scoffing and answering. She let the pause do what words couldn't.

"I've been there," Sophia said, voice low. "The 3 a.m. emails, the pristine decks, the meetings where your idea lands better when someone else says it. I used to think that was the win. But you've already got the title, the reputation, the seat. You don't have to keep proving it, Ava. When do you actually get to live?"

Ava's vision blurred. Heat built behind her eyes, but she pushed it down. *Who the hell does she think she is?*

Sophia tilted her head, studying her. "You've built everything you were supposed to. So why does it still look like it's costing you everything?"

The words landed harder than Ava wanted them to. She straightened, slipping the persona back on. "I'm fine. It's just been a long week."

Sophia studied her for a moment, like she could see past the perfect hair and practiced smile to whatever was fraying underneath. "That look in your eyes," she said finally. "I've seen it before... in me. It's what you get when you're running so fast you forget where you were headed."

Ava's throat cinched shut. She reached for a joke, a deflection, anything to buy her escape, but the words refused to come.

Sophia's tone softened. "Just... think about it. A few of us are going to this women's retreat. No panels, no speeches, no networking, no performance. Just time away with women who get it. You could be my plus-one if you want."

Sophia smirked as she headed for the door. "Don't roll your eyes until you've tried it. Call me!" Her heels struck the tile, the scent of jasmine following in her wake.

Ava stood in the bathroom alone, staring at her reflection in the gold-framed mirror. Same hair. Same suit. Same woman who walked in five minutes ago.

So why did she suddenly feel like a stranger to herself?

She returned to the table with her armor back on. Smiled through dessert. Laughed at the right moments. No one noticed she'd left. No one noticed she'd come back.

By the time she made it home, it was past eleven. She kicked off her heels and stood in her kitchen, the silence louder than the restaurant had been.

Her running shoes sat by the door, laces still tied from this morning. She hadn't made it to the gym in four days, but she'd promised herself she'd go tomorrow. The treadmill was her therapy—the only place she could outrun the noise in her head.

The next morning, Ava's eyes opened at 4:15 without an alarm. Habit. Market hours had trained her body clock better than any iPhone could.

She lay still for a moment, staring at the ceiling, last night's dinner replaying in her mind: Tom's gaze sliding past her, David's backhanded praise, Sophia's question. *"When's the last time you did something because you wanted to?"*

She pushed the thought aside and reached for her phone. She scrolled through overnight emails, mentally sorting them into urgent, can-wait, and dead-on-arrival.

This was supposed to be the dream. The corner office. The seven-figure portfolio. The kind of arrival that made other women ask her to coffee to "pick her brain."

So why did it feel like she was performing her own life?

By 4:30 a.m., she was in workout gear. The gym was her church: treadmill at 6.5 mph, incline at eight, exactly forty-five minutes. The rhythm was mindless. Lately, so was the work. She kept wondering if the next opportunity would just be more of the same—another title, another portfolio, another win that felt like nothing.

The first twenty minutes were a blur of footfalls and mental to-do lists: Singapore held, Westridge needed a volatility brief, Henderson dinner follow-up. She jabbed at her podcast queue, hovering skip before landing on a featured title: *The Invisible Rulebook.*

A woman's voice filled her earbuds, warm but deliberate, like she was letting Ava in on something she'd only say to a friend.

"No one hands you this rulebook, but if you're a high-achieving woman, you know it exists. This isn't about blame—it's about seeing what's been hidden in plain sight. The game was built long before you arrived, and the rules were never written with your freedom in mind."

Ava's pace didn't slow, but her breath caught, ragged against the rhythm of her feet.

"Be confident—but not too direct. Work twice as hard just to be seen as competent. Look effortless but make it flawless. Lead, but don't you dare want the power. And if you stumble, they'll say you were never meant to play the game at all."

A laugh escaped—short, bitter. She didn't need a podcast to tell her the rules. She'd been breathing them in for years.

"These rules aren't written down, which makes them harder to question. They seep in through what gets praised, what gets ignored, and what gets quietly punished. They start to feel like truth—until one day, you realize they're only rules

you never agreed to. And in that moment, you have a choice: keep playing by them or begin again on your own terms."

Ava's stride faltered, just slightly. The podcast guest's words threaded through her mind, tangling with the memory of Tom looking past her as if she were part of the décor.

It wasn't just about being overlooked. It was the slow, grinding realization that the work no longer lit her up. She was still delivering wins, but the fire that used to pull her into the office before sunrise had burned down to embers.

The incline beeped higher. Ava pushed harder.

Ava was halfway down the hallway toward her building's elevators when her phone buzzed. The name on the screen stopped her mid-step.

Emma.

She swiped to answer, lifting her voice into something bright. "Hey, baby girl."

"Auntie Ava!" The excitement in Emma's voice was immediate. "Guess what? My play was last night."

Ava felt it start in the pit of her stomach. "I know, sweetie. How did it go?"

"It was so good. I got to yell a lot because Miss Trunchbull is mean, and everyone laughed when I stomped my feet." A quick inhale. "Mom said you couldn't come 'cause you had a big dinner thing."

Ava leaned against the wall, palm pressed flat, like she needed the drywall to hold her up. "I'm sorry I missed it. I bet you were amazing."

"Yeah," Emma said matter-of-factly, "but it's more fun when you're there."

A breath passed. Then, in a softer voice, Emma said, "Were you sad? You didn't sound happy when you called to say good luck."

The question wasn't an accusation, just curiosity, but it lodged under Ava's ribs. "Oh, honey... no. I just had a lot on my mind."

"Okay," Emma said, stretching the word like she was filing the answer away. "I love you."

"I love you too. More than anything."

The line clicked dead, leaving Ava alone in the hallway.

She stared at the phone a moment longer, thumb resting where the end call button had been, the screen already dark. The air in the hallway felt heavier, like it was pressing her into the wall.

It wasn't just missing the play. It was missing that look—the one Emma flashed Ava when she spotted her in the crowd, the little wave she tried to hide so her friends wouldn't see. Ava could picture it perfectly, could almost feel the warm flush of love and pride that came with it.

She'd traded Emma's play for a table where she might as well have been an empty chair.

Her inner voice was merciless: *Of course, you showed up here. And, of course, it meant not showing up there.*

She rubbed the base of her neck—the motion automatic—a tell she couldn't quiet disguise.

She could run numbers, forecast outcomes, and calculate risk for clients all day. But there was no model for the damage of missed moments like Emma's play. No formula for how many you could skip before the people you love stop counting on you.

She walked toward the elevator. Her reflection in the metal doors looked crisp, professional, every hair in place. The kind of woman who made the hard calls. The kind who didn't let a child's disappointment derail her.

So why did it feel like she'd just lost the deal that mattered most—and it had nothing to do with a client's portfolio?

The doors slid open on her office floor, and Ava stepped out with Emma's voice echoing in her mind.

By the time she reached her desk, the day had already swallowed her whole. Back-to-back Zoom calls blurred together—updates, reviews, "quick touch bases" that never ended when they were supposed to.

Claire, her assistant, pinged her mid-meeting about a fire drill. A manager somewhere was suddenly "concerned about optics." Another team wanted changes at the last second. Urgent, of course. Her lunch wilted on the counter, avocado browning, vinaigrette bleeding through the plastic lid. At 2:15 p.m., she muted her line to force down two bites of rubbery chicken before the next meeting.

By 4 p.m., her voice was raw. By 6 p.m., her camera smile felt stapled in place. The pressure wasn't sneaking up on her; it had been living under her skin all day. She told herself she'd call her mom to check in after the last meeting, but it bled into another "quick one" that ran long, like they always did. Her only break was walking from her desk to the kitchen for water twice, and even then, she answered emails on her phone.

When she finally logged off, it was 9:07 p.m. Her eyes ached from the glow of her screen. Her to-do list was longer than it had been that morning. Tom's dinner follow-up was still waiting, but she didn't have the energy to pretend anyone was her priority tonight. She slipped her laptop into her bag, pretending it meant the day was done. She knew better. The work never stayed put; it just multiplied overnight.

She carried the day home with her, every meeting and missed moment pressed into her shoulders as she unlocked her apartment door. Inside, everything was silent. The space was immaculate, every surface gleaming, every piece of furniture exactly where it belonged.

She dropped her bag on the counter and stood there a moment, taking it in. Perfect. Ordered. And still, she felt like a guest in her own life. She kicked off her heels, pausing beside the untouched bottle of wine she'd bought two weeks ago. She was saving it for a moment worth opening.

That day still hadn't come.

Her phone sat in her hand, heavier than it should have been. She opened the voice memo app, thumb hovering over the red button. She always recorded at night—pep talks, debriefs, notes for tomorrow's to-do list. She almost never listened to them again. It was just a way to convince herself she was moving forward.

The red circle glowed. She hit record.

"Okay," she muttered under her breath. "Day's done. Deals moved forward, money was made, boxes were checked. Westridge didn't see it coming, and David did his little 'let me explain' routine again. Whatever. It plays well in the room." Her gaze drifted to city lights, sharp against the glass. "And Emma's play... well, she'll have more. Kids bounce back. I'll make the next one. No one remembers every single play anyway."

Her shoulders inched toward her ears, the knot at the base of her neck pulsing. She forced them down, back into place, as if control over her body might translate into control over everything else.

"This is what success looks like: long days, missed dinners, the trade-offs. Everyone at this level does it. Everyone sacrifices. You're not special. Get over it. This is the job. This is the deal. And I should be grateful to even have it."

The thought flickered—maybe this wasn't what "making it" was supposed to feel like. She killed it fast, the way she always did.

Easier to call it the deal than admit the cost.

Her laugh was short, without humor. "If anyone else said that, I'd roll my eyes. But here I am explaining it away. Again."

The room felt smaller now. She was still carrying the day with her, too tired to pretend otherwise. Everything around her was perfect, but it didn't feel like her. She'd spent years building a life that looked impressive, not one that felt alive.

And even now, sitting in her home, she felt less like the woman who paid the mortgage and more like someone waiting to be told she'd overstayed her welcome.

It wasn't just her condo. It was the life she'd built to afford it—the exhaustion no amount of sleep could cure, the calendar packed so tight that there was no room for joy unless it was scheduled weeks in advance. The salary didn't make her powerful. It made her obedient.

She'd built it all, piece by piece, deal by deal—only to realize the fortress was also a prison.

She'd mistaken the ache for drive, the numbness for focus. They called it ambition. She called it survival.

"What the hell am I doing?" she murmured, almost forgetting the memo was still recording.

She stared at *delete* like it was a trap she kept setting for herself.

But she didn't press it. Not tonight.

She saved the voice memo instead, the truth sealed inside her phone like evidence she wasn't ready to destroy.

The Invisible Load
*the unpaid work that funds
everyone else's dreams*

FROM THE OUTSIDE, SARAH'S LIFE LOOKED LIKE THE GOAL. THE house was tastefully decorated—linen drapes, reclaimed wood floors, eucalyptus arranged just so in a ceramic vase by the window.

Her kids went to a private school with a waitlist. Her husband had a multiple six-figure salary. The fridge was always stocked with organic oat milk and grass-fed butter. Even their dog, Cooper, had a rotation of gingham bandanas.

She lived in the kind of neighborhood where women wore matching athleisure to Pilates and carried Stanley cups the size of their toddlers. Where the group chat was a steady stream of recipe swaps, birthday RSVPs, and quiet comparisons no one ever admitted making.

Sometimes, she caught herself looking around and wondering whose life she was actually living.

Once, she'd felt proud of what she'd built—maybe even lucky. But lately, it all felt less like a dream and more like a beautiful cage.

Sarah woke before her alarm, as she always did. For a few fleeting seconds, everything felt still. Hopeful, even. Morning light spilled through the window like a promise, softening the sharp corners of her room. She imagined brewing coffee alone,

stepping outside barefoot to breathe in the cool air, maybe jour-
naling before the house stirred awake. Maybe today would feel
different.

She pictured what it might be like to have time to herself—to
be a woman who wasn't always the last priority on her own list.
Just one slow hour.

She used to have a morning ritual. Now she just had mornings. The house was quiet, but not peaceful. A journal sat on
the counter, the pages still blank. A yoga mat stayed rolled in
the closet. Notifications flickered across her phone: a missed call
from her sister Kendra, the school newsletter, an Amazon deliv-
ery alert. Then one subject line made her pause: *"Reimagine
What's Next."*

The email had landed in her inbox three days ago—probably
from some blog she'd subscribed to during one of those late-
night rabbit holes on *finding yourself* or *simplifying life.* She
couldn't remember which.

She opened it without thinking. The first lines were bold but
gentle:

*"You built a life around the people you love. The house that
runs because of you. The calendar only you can keep straight.
The meals, the rides, the endless little things no one else sees.
From the outside, it looks steady, even enviable."*

Blue light flickered across her face, waiting for her to decide.

*"You became the strong one—the one who made sure every-
one else was okay, even when you weren't. And beneath the
carefully constructed life, a quieter question stirs: When did
I stop showing up for myself?"*

Something in her chest shifted—small, but unmistakable. It was as if the email saw her in a way even her closest friends couldn't.

At the bottom, one simple line waited: *"Begin again, from here."*

She didn't click it. *When I'm ready.*

Down the hall, small feet hit the floor—the morning already pulling her back into its current.

The checklist rebuilt itself: lunchboxes, soccer gear, a missing library book, a quick browse through Pottery Barn, and the dry cleaning. Always the damn dry cleaning.

By 7:15 a.m., she stood in her spotless kitchen, assembling school lunches.

"Turkey, apple slices, and string cheese on repeat. Every. Single. Day."

Her voice sounded mechanical, like someone running through a routine she didn't have to think about anymore. In the microwave's reflection: a messy bun, no makeup, the same gray Beyond Yoga hoodie she'd worn all week. She exhaled, the sigh landing somewhere between fatigue and acceptance.

Ethan looked up from his phone, coffee in hand. "Did you grab the dry cleaning?"

Sarah rolled her eyes. "It's on my list for today—right after my drop offs."

He glanced back at his screen. "I need the blue shirt for tomorrow."

She kept slicing apples. "Then I'll make it happen," she said, flat.

Ethan didn't comment on the edge in her voice. Maybe he didn't hear it. Maybe he didn't care to.

She wiped apple juice from the counter with more force than necessary.

"So, about movie night with the kids—"

Ethan looked up again, guilt flickering across his face before he turned away. "I got caught up with the Peterson account. You know how it is."

"I know exactly how it is," Sarah said, eyes on the cutting board. "Which is also why I sat through the PTA meeting alone too. Our kids' lives keep happening, Ethan—whether you show up or not."

The silence lingered between them until Olivia, their nine-year-old, bounced into the kitchen—ending a conversation that was never going anywhere anyway.

"This shirt is itchy and stupid, and I hate it!" she screamed, throwing the shirt on the floor.

Sarah took a deep breath before responding. "You liked it last night when you picked it out, remember?"

Olivia placed her hands on her narrow hips and scowled. "Well, I changed my mind." It was like watching a miniature version of herself unravel, same eyes, same fire, same stubborn defiance. Sarah got it—too well—which was probably why it stung.

Olivia marched over to the counter like a drill sergeant inspecting a cadet's work.

"Madison has cheese squares in her lunch, not string cheese," she announced, arms crossed, like this was a gross maternal oversight.

"Of course she does," Sarah muttered under her breath.

"What?" Olivia snapped, already suspicious.

"Nothing, honey," Sarah said, wiping her brow. "String cheese is perfectly fine. It's what we've got, and it's already packed."

Olivia wagged a finger at her mother, full of secondhand authority. "Madison's mom says string cheese has per-sur-tives in it, and it's not good for you."

Sarah froze, a half-made sandwich in her hands.

"You mean preservatives?" she asked, raising an eyebrow. "It literally says no artificial preservatives right here on the label."

Olivia folded her arms. "Yeah, but it's not the fancy kind of cheese."

Sarah glanced at Ethan for backup, but his eyes were still glued to his phone. When he finally looked up, he just shrugged like Olivia was speaking in riddles or French. Of course, she was on her own. Again.

Their five-year-old son, Ben, bounced into the room, clutching his plastic T-Rex like a prized possession. "Mommy! Can Rex come to school with me?"

Ethan lowered his coffee mug, not bothering to hide his sigh. "No dinosaurs at school, Ben. You're five now," he said, like that should explain everything.

Sarah started gently, "Actually, his teacher said—"

"Sarah, he's five. He needs to learn boundaries," Ethan cut in, already frowning.

Sarah hesitated, lips parted, then let it go. "Right. Boundaries," she murmured, returning to the lunch boxes as if the comment didn't sting. But it did.

"Mom?" Olivia tugged at her sleeve, eyes wide. "Can you braid my hair now?"

Sarah didn't look up. "In a second, baby."

Ethan glanced up, brows pulled together in a look meant to pass for concern.

"You look tired. Maybe try going to bed earlier."

Sarah met his comment midair.

"Yeah. Maybe I just need more sleep. That'll fix everything."

His tone sharpened. "I'm just saying—"

"I know what you're saying," she cut in, voice calm but clipped. "It's just not realistic."

The quiet tension stretched—too long to be comfortable, too familiar to be surprising.

Ethan went back to scrolling.

She turned back to the cutting board, not because there was more to do but because it was easier than saying what she really needed.

She picked up her phone and reread the email line—*Reimagine What's Next*—as if, this time, it might unlock something.

She drew in a slow breath, eyes still on the screen. *Right. I wouldn't even know where to start.*

"Mom!" Olivia screamed from down the hall. Sarah locked her phone screen, not closing the email but tucking it away. She wasn't ready to delete it.

"I'm coming, Liv," she called, pushing herself away from the counter.

They headed to the upstairs bathroom. Sarah reached for a brush and began braiding Olivia's hair with the kind of practiced ease that came from doing it every morning—same routine, same soft tangles, same fingers moving without thought.

"There. Perfect."

She met Olivia's eyes in the mirror and offered a tired but tender smile. Olivia studied her reflection for a moment, lips pursed like she was searching for something.

"Mom, do you think I'm as pretty as you?"

The question caught Sarah mid-braid. She looked at her daughter's reflection—not just her face, but the lightness she still carried. The unfiltered confidence. The willingness to ask what Sarah had learned to swallow.

Sarah rested her hands on Olivia's shoulders, steadying them both.

"I think you're everything I want to remember."

Olivia frowned. "Huh?"

Sarah smiled, brushing a loose strand behind her ear.

"It means yes, baby. You're beautiful."

She said it softly, almost a whisper—more wish than answer. The words were meant for Olivia, but they brushed against something in her too. A reminder to see herself, not just the reflection she'd learn to maintain.

When Olivia skipped off toward the hallway, the braid swaying behind her, Sarah stayed where she was, fingers still tingling from the weight of her daughter's hair. In the mirror, she caught her own eyes—resigned, searching—and for the briefest second, she saw the woman her daughter must see. Then the moment passed.

She exhaled, turned off the light, and followed the sound of Olivia's footsteps down the hall.

By 8:45 a.m., Sarah sat idling in the school drop-off line, her Acura MDX wedged between a black Range Rover and a silver Mercedes GLS.

She'd gone with the "sensible" choice when Ethan got promoted—only later did she realize she'd become the mom without ambient lighting or a logo that turned heads.

The irony wasn't lost on her. She had everything she'd once wanted – everything she was supposed to want - yet somehow she was always rushing, chasing, without ever arriving anywhere that felt like hers.

She found a parking spot a minute later, pulled in, and turned around to face the back seat.

"Okay, Liv, grab your backpack. Ben, T-Rex gets to stay in the car today."

"But T-Rex wants to say goodbye, too!" Ben wailed, clutching the plastic dinosaur like it was a limb.

Sarah closed her eyes for half a second and pressed two fingers to her temple.

"He can wave from the car," she said, voice flat but firm.

Olivia was already sighing about something else—her jacket too warm, her backpack strap twisted again.

Sarah barely registered which complaint it was this time. She just opened the door and stepped into the chill morning air.

Voices overlapped. A backpack strap snagged. Someone tripped, someone laughed. Car doors thudded shut behind her, one after another, until the noise dissolved into morning traffic.

Sarah locked her car with a tap, not noticing the faint shape in the rearview mirror as she turned toward the school. The day was already tugging her forward.

Sarah spotted Marissa near the school entrance and felt that familiar mix of relief and dread.

Marissa was in her usual uniform—high-waisted leggings, a cashmere wrap, hair that somehow looked styled even in a ponytail. She held a green smoothie like an accessory, the kind of effortless that required effort. Not a hair out of place. Not a stain in sight.

She had the kind of presence that could make you feel both welcome and wildly behind on your life.

Marissa waved them over. Sarah fell into step beside Olivia, joining the slow drift of families funneling toward the entrance— the small tide of backpacks and coffee cups that marked the start of another day.

"Sarah! How are you?" Marissa called, her grin bright and camera-ready.

"Good! Just... you know. The usual morning fire drill."

Marissa laughed—light, effortless. "I'm jealous. You're so lucky you get to just focus on family. I was up 'til midnight finishing a pitch deck."

She took a slow sip of her smoothie, eyes sparkling. "Seriously, though, what do you even do with all that free time? I'd kill for a day without meetings."

Sarah's fingers grasped Olivia's backpack strap before she even realized she was holding it. Her smile followed, tightening almost imperceptibly.

Free time.

She'd been up since the crack of dawn, packed two lunches, diffused a wardrobe crisis, and mentally cataloged seventeen things that needed to happen before noon.

But there was no conference call. No presentation. No moment when someone would lean forward and say, "Sarah, what do you think?"

Just motion. Endless motion. Without momentum.

"Free time. Right." Sarah adjusted her purse strap—a Kate Spade bag from her working days, now filled with Goldfish crackers and wet wipes instead of business cards.

She forced a smile.

"Yeah. Lucky me."

The words soured as soon as they left her mouth. *Lucky. Right. I should feel lucky.*

Beautiful kids. Nice house. A husband with a steady job.

The life she'd built was full, framed, finished—and she'd blurred somewhere in the middle.

Marissa didn't seem to notice the pause.

"Oh! I'm speaking at that women's leadership summit next month. Can you believe it? So surreal. You never know what doors open when you stay in the game."

Sarah swallowed. Something thick caught in her throat, a feeling she couldn't quite name.

She smiled. Nodded. Said nothing.

Olivia tugged at her sleeve. "Mom, can I go?"

Before Sarah could respond, Marissa's smile brightened. "Madison! Come say hi to Mrs. Greene!"

Madison bounced over, all high ponytail and practiced charm.

"Hi, Mrs. Greene!" she chirped. Then to Olivia: "My mom's giving a big speech about women leaders."

Olivia shrugged. "My mom doesn't give speeches."

The words hit harder than they should have. Sarah pressed her lips together, keeping her face neutral, though something inside her folded a little more.

Marissa chimed in, voice bright. "Well, your mom has the most important job of all—being your mommy!"

To Sarah, it felt like a pat on the head. Well-meant, but dismissive.

"I should get going, Marissa." Her smile was thin. "Good seeing you."

Marissa beamed. "Of course! Enjoy your day off!" She turned and walked off, arm draped around Madison.

Sarah watched them go, wondering how some women made it all look easy when it never really was.

Olivia squinted up at Sarah, blinking against the morning sun.

"Mom? Why don't you go to work like Madison's mom?"

Sarah stiffened. "What do you mean?"

"You don't have a job. You're just a mom."

Sarah's shoulders tensed. Her voice stayed calm—too calm. "Taking care of you is my job."

Olivia frowned, thinking.

"But Madison's mom said it's not a real job if you don't get paid."

Sarah felt the words land—small, sharp, and unfairly familiar. She didn't answer. She knelt to zip Olivia's jacket, smoothing the fabric with hands that suddenly felt unsteady.

"Go on, honey. You don't want to be late."

"Okay! Love you!" Olivia called, already skipping toward the school.

Sarah waved back but didn't move.

The smile stayed fixed, the way everything did when she didn't have the energy to fall apart.

She watched Olivia disappear into the school building, her daughter's words still lingering like steam on glass.

Stay-at-home moms don't have a job.

Sarah turned toward the parking lot, trying to shake it off. *It's fine. I'm fine. I chose this.*

She straightened her posture. Lifted her chin. *Gratitude is everything. You're lucky. You're grounded. This is sacred work. Women would kill for this.*

The words were supposed to steady her. But by the time she reached the car, the pep talk already felt stale—like trying to sell herself on a job she didn't even want.

She opened the car door—

"Mommy! T-Rex says thank you for letting him wave from the car!" Ben shouted, triumphant.

Sarah jolted, hand flying to her chest as her heart slammed against her ribs.

"Shit—Ben! I forgot you were—"

The words broke off. Her hands shook as she gripped the doorframe. *What kind of mother forgets her own child in the back seat?*

Panic surged, cold and sharp. *What if he'd gotten out on the street? What if—*

"That's a bad word, Mommy!" Ben squealed from the back seat, blissfully unaware.

Sarah forced her breathing to slow, willing her pulse to follow.

"You're right, peanut. I'm sorry."

She slid into the driver's seat, fingers still trembling as she adjusted the rearview mirror.

"Let's get you to school."

Later that morning, Sarah stood in her spotless kitchen. The dishwasher clicked on, and the house was finally quiet.

She should have felt relief. Instead, she felt the familiar restlessness pressing against her ribs—the kind that made her reach for tasks that didn't need doing.

She wiped down the already-clean bathroom showers. Reorganized the junk drawer. Straightened the mail pile by the door.

That's when she saw it: a folder she'd meant to file months ago, wedged between crumpled receipts, and a stack of unopened mail. Her old career folder—the one she'd kept meaning to scan and store properly but never had the energy for.

Sarah pulled it free, the weight of it surprising her—like she'd forgotten it still existed.

She opened it slowly. Inside were performance reviews, project summaries, a letter of recommendation from her old boss.

And then, tucked between two pages, a printout she'd forgotten existed.

"Reimagining Work as a Place of Belonging"
By Sarah Greene
DRAFT – June 2016

Her breath caught.

She remembered writing this. Late at night, weeks before Olivia was born, when she was still convinced that she'd return to work differently—not harder, but wiser. She'd been so full of ideas back then, so certain she had something important to say.

Sarah leaned against the counter and began to read.

"What if we stopped treating work-life balance like a zero-sum game? What if belonging wasn't about fitting into someone else's system but about building systems where people could thrive without disappearing?"

The words were hers. Clear. Confident. Unguarded.

She kept reading, faster now, pulled in by the voice on the page—a woman who believed her perspective mattered, who trusted herself to put ideas into the world without asking permission first.

"Retention isn't a benefits problem. It's a belonging problem. And until we create workplaces where people can show up fully—not just productively but humanly—we'll keep losing the talent we claim to value most."

Sarah pressed her lips together.

This was me. This woman knew things. Had opinions. Took up space.

She read to the end—three pages that stopped mid-thought, as if she'd been interrupted and never returned.

The essay was good. Really good.

And that hit her like cold water: she'd buried this voice under the noise of everyone else's needs.

She stood there, papers in hand, recognizing the woman she used to be—the one who spoke up without apology, who didn't wait for someone else to say she was right.

The woman on that page would never have asked permission to matter.

Sarah flipped the pages. She wanted to feel angry—at Ethan, at Marissa, at the expectations that made her choice feel like a duty. But all she felt was tired. And under that, something quieter. A knowing maybe—that she'd slowly faded herself out.

Sarah folded the pages carefully and slid them back into the folder.

Not today.

But this time, she didn't hide them either.

"Another day, just me and my sweet boy Cooper," she said, rubbing his ears with both hands. His fur slipped through her fingers, warm and steadying.

He pressed against her leg, and for a second she let herself be still. Then the stillness got loud.

She picked up her phone, her finger tracing the edge of the screen. Who was she even going to text—her husband about not being home late? The school group chat about spirit-day outfits? She set it down again with a sigh.

Once upon a time, her mornings were filled with HR strategy calls and change management milestones, people waiting on her opinion. She'd worked like hell in her twenties, made VP before thirty, told herself she was doing it all so she could *choose* to stay home someday. And she did.

Not because she couldn't handle the hustle—she'd practically built her career on it—but because she remembered coming home to an empty house. Her mom always working. Always tired. Sarah had grown up watching her equate love in leftovers and late nights, promising herself she'd never make her kids feel like second place.

She'd sworn it would be different for her kids. And it was. She was there for every pickup, every game, every last-minute art project. Her presence was the thing she'd traded everything else for.

"Alexa," she said, "do I have any meetings today?"

"You have no events scheduled."

Sarah tilted her head. "Tomorrow?"

"You have no events scheduled."

She laughed once—a dry, half breath.

"No events. No plans. No place to be."

A pause. Then, lighter: "Love that for me."

She picked up her phone, the screen lighting her face as her hand fell into its usual scroll.

Three new posts since drop-off: Madison's art project, a "Power Mommy Morning Routine," and a family selfie from the beach.

"Seriously, does Marissa ever stop posting?" Sarah muttered. Then came the guilt—sharp and automatic. Maybe she should be posting more.

She opened her camera roll and started scrolling.

Ben's first day of kindergarten. Olivia's soccer games. Kids smiling. Kids crying. Kids sleeping.

All of it: them.

She paused. Tilted her head.

"When did I stop being in pictures?" she asked, not expecting an answer.

Scrolling again, she finally found one—a family photo from last year.

She was half cut off, wearing a stretched-out sweatshirt, mid-blink, mouth open, caught in motion. The only one she'd been in for months. And even there, she wasn't really in it.

Sarah stared a bit longer, then locked her phone. She caught her reflection in the black TV screen. "I used to wear real pants," she muttered. "With buttons."

A dry laugh escaped. People at work used to ask what she thought about things that didn't involve snacks or screen time. Now she knew more about TikTok parenting hacks than the new hybrid-work guidelines.

She reached for her journal—the one she'd found on a parenting blog for Mindful Mommies. She'd written in it three times. Maybe four. Still, today felt like one of those days.

She opened to a blank page, stared, and finally wrote: *I used to be funny. At least, people laughed. I used to matter, too. I think. I think. I used to matter.* She left the journal open—emotional growth could wait—and grabbed her phone. Time for something easier. She tapped FaceTime and called her sister, Kendra.

"Sarah! Hey! I literally have two minutes before my next meeting."

Sarah smiled. "You look great. New haircut?"

Kendra leaned in and winked. "Yep—It Girl cut. Total boss energy." She tilted her head. "You look... tired. Are you sleeping?"

"I'm fine," Sarah said, smile fixed in place.

Kendra squinted. "Try that dry shampoo I sent you. Or maybe just... a brush?"

Sarah gave the peacekeeping laugh. "Right. Thanks."

Kendra glanced at another screen. "What's up today?"

"Just thought I'd check in," Sarah said. "It's been a while."

Kendra groaned. "Ugh, chaos. Milan's behind, the fall campaign's on fire. You're lucky—no deadlines, no politics. Just domestic bliss, right?"

Sarah raised an eyebrow. "Yeah. Bliss."

"Don't roll your eyes," Kendra said without looking up. "Seriously—hot husband, healthy kids, no work drama? I'd trade places in a second."

Sarah wandered the house. "I've been thinking about doing something new. Maybe coaching or consulting—leadership, strategy, that kind of thing."

Kendra laughed. "You and your phases. What was that book you made us read in Cabo? The Power of... something?"

"The Power of Habit," Sarah said.

"Marcus!" Kendra yelled off-screen. "No—matte finish, not high gloss!"

She turned back, distracted smile already fading. "I want to hear more, but this campaign's in rescue mode and my next meeting's starting. I'll call you later—love you, bye!"

The screen went black. Sarah's eyes drifted across the room, landing on the fridge.

A crumpled piece of construction paper was hanging there with a magnet shaped like a cat. It was a drawing—marker lines, triangle dresses, lopsided smiles. "Me and Mom," written in Olivia's backward E.

Sarah stepped closer. She was in the picture. Centered. Holding hands. Smiling—the way Olivia saw her. Not background. Not invisible. Just... Mom.

She smiled. "Well, at least someone remembers who I am."

"Alexa," she said, still looking at the picture. "Remind me to buy more markers."

"Adding markers to your shopping list," Alexa chirped.

Sarah laughed quietly. "Good start."

Maybe they'd spend the afternoon drawing together.

Later after dinner, Sarah stood at the sink, drying her hands, watching the last light fade through the window.

From the living room came the clatter of LEGOs and the soft voice of a children's audiobook— the kind of sound that let her shoulders finally drop.

She didn't realize she was smiling until she caught her reflection in the dark window. Hard to believe the same house could feel so different when it was just her.

"Mom! Can we watch the dino movie again after bath?" Ben shouted from the top of the stairs.

"Sure," she called back. "After teeth."

"Can we have popcorn like Daddy's movie night?" Olivia chimed in.

Sarah turned. "Daddy's movie night?"

"Yeah," Olivia said brightly. "Last Friday, when you went to your book thing. We stayed up late and had root beer floats!"

"And we got to eat on the couch!" Ben added.

Sarah grinned. "Root beer floats, huh? I see how it is. Tonight I'm calling it Mom's Movie Marathon—with real ice cream, not the healthy kind."

"Can we?!" Olivia's voice rang through the house. Ben's footsteps thudded overhead. "Yeah! With popcorn!" Sarah laughed, the kind that reached her belly this time. For a brief stretch, the fatigue of the day melted.

The kids raced downstairs, giggling and breathless, and tossed a bag of popcorn in the microwave. They got distracted—playing, laughing, bouncing—and forgot to take it out in time. The sharp smell of burnt kernels filled the kitchen.

Ben's face crumpled. "It's ruined!" he wailed. "Rex wanted popcorn too!"

Sarah knelt beside him, calm and steady. "I get it. Burnt snacks are basically a tragedy when you're five. Total devastation."

Ben sniffled. "And now Rex is sad."

She grabbed another bag from the cabinet and slid it into the microwave. "Let's try again. This time, we listen for the pops. Deal?"

"Deal," he said, tears already drying.

They crouched together in front of the microwave, counting the seconds between bursts.

"Careful," she whispered. "If we're quiet, we can catch the popcorn doing its magic trick."

Ben giggled. "It's like magic!"

Olivia leaned in beside them. "Popcorn magic!"

Sarah pulled the steaming bag free, poured it into a bowl, and pressed it gently into Ben's hands.

He grinned, wide and pleased. Olivia slipped in beside him, steadying the bowl with her small, careful hands as she led him to the family room.

Their giggles drifted back through the hall, soft and innocent, the kind of sound that made her whole body unclench.

When she joined them on the couch, she just watched them – her whole heart walking around outside her body, alive with joy.

The rest of the evening blurred in small rituals – bedtime stories, lights clicked off, a last glass of water.

By 9:00 p.m., the house had gone still. Sarah walked into the bedroom, towel around her torso, lotion on her hands, hair damp, robe tied loosely at her waist.

Ethan was already in bed, propped against a stack of pillows—laptop open, phone in hand. Dinner had come and gone without him—again.

Sarah climbed in slowly, iPad in hand. She waited—for a glance, a word, anything – but nothing came.

She fluffed her pillow and tried anyway.

"The kids had a blast tonight," she said lightly. "We ended up having an impromptu movie night. They said you let them do popcorn on the couch."

"Yeah, sorry I missed it." Ethan murmured, eyes still on the screen. "I meant to leave on time—today just got away from me."

"You missed quite a show," she said. "Ben tried to share popcorn with Cooper and ended up in full negotiation."

Ethan's mouth curved faintly. "That's cute. Tell the kids we'll do it another time."

His eyes never left the screen.

Sarah watched him for a few seconds. "They won't believe me," she said quietly. "They're starting to learn what 'another time' means."

Ethan exhaled, rubbing his temple. "Sarah, come on. I'm doing my best here."

Her voice stayed even. "Are you?"

He looked up then—defensive, tired. "I'm working. For all of us."

Years ago, they'd agreed—he'd focus on his career, she'd hold down everything else. For awhile, it worked.

"I know," she said, tucking the blanket over her legs. "It just feels like we're all waiting for you to be done working and actually *here*."

That got his attention. He turned, annoyed. "What's that supposed to mean?"

She looked away. "It means... never mind."

She opened her iPad. Scrolled. Tapped. Stopped.

Ethan's tone sharpened. "If something's wrong, just say it."

Sarah set the iPad down. "You know, I try. But when I do, I'm either dramatic, needy, too sensitive—take your pick."

Ethan rolled his eyes. "Here we go."

She didn't flinch. "It's a thing, Ethan. You just don't notice because you don't have to."

He snapped his laptop shut and sat up. "Okay, what exactly do you want from me right now?"

Her face softened—not in surrender, but in exhaustion.

"I don't know," she said. "Just...ask me something that isn't about the kids or logistics. Like you still see *me*."

Ethan stared. "That's not fair."

Sarah tilted her head. "Neither is being invisible in your own damn marriage."

That landed. He exhaled—the fight leaving his body, replaced by something that looked a lot like regret.

For a stretch, they just looked at each other—two people separated by the same quiet they'd both helped build.

"You want to talk this through?" he asked finally.

Sarah glanced down at her hands, faintly scented from lotion. "No. I'm good."

He nodded once, then climbed out of bed without another word. Cooper seized the opportunity to take his spot. As she stroked his fur, Sarah listened to the dull rhythm of footsteps fading down the hall, then the soft click of Ethan's office door.

She reached for the screen—habit, not comfort. Better to scroll than to say something she couldn't take back.

Hallmark movie? Reality show? Maybe a recipe blog or Kendra's new campaign photo feed. Anything easy. Anything that wouldn't open the floodgates. But none of it could touch the quiet she was sitting in—the kind that seeps in when a marriage starts to run on autopilot.

She remembered the email from that morning: *Reimagine What's Next.*

She hesitated. The argument still lingered—small words, sharp edges, the kind that leave bruises no one can see. She wasn't sure she had it in her to look inward tonight.

But she skimmed, a line caught her eye—bold and simple:

"Where have you been holding it all together at the expense of yourself? And when was the last time you made a choice that was fully yours?"

Sarah stared at the screen, something in her chest loosening. Not hope, exactly. Just...recognition. Like someone had finally named the thing she'd been carrying for awhile.

She kept reading:

"You already know what isn't working. Now it's time to see what's really going on— and what to do about it."

Something in her shifted. It wasn't the usual gloss of most self-help emails. It was quieter. Clearer. Like it had been written by someone who understood what it meant to live between two versions of herself.

She scrolled further.

"The filters that matter most: your values, your energy, your legacy and your impact. Start there."

Sarah stared at the phrase: *what's really going on—and what to do about it.*

That was it. The question she'd been chasing without even knowing it. Something that didn't ask her to try so hard.

Somewhere deep inside —the part of her that used to know what she wanted—something woke up. She wasn't ready to move. But she finally stopped pretending she couldn't feel it.

The Good Daughter

*when managing wealth
replaces living well*

Everything around Grace gleamed with the proof of a good life. But none of it settled in her bones.

She wasn't sure what she was searching for—clarity, distraction, a sign—but her fingers moved on her keyboard anyway. *Legacy planning events. Women and wealth.* It sounded ridiculous even as she typed it, but she hit search anyway.

The results loaded in a predictable blur: white-toothed male advisors, stock photo couples laughing over dinner on some posh cruise deck. It all looked like the world her father came up in—orderly, masculine, impenetrable.

And yet, as she scrolled, something in her resisted.

She paused on a headline she almost missed.

"Whole Woman Wealth"

The homepage didn't look like every other financial site. Calmer somehow. Less aggressive. It caught her off guard—who makes wealth look *warm*?

She clicked before she could overthink it.

The site loaded. Simple. Direct. No section titled "For Women Investors" like she needed a separate, simpler version.

Near the bottom of the page, a single line caught her eye:

"The Rich Like Her Manifesto"

The line didn't try to convince her of anything. It just...was.

"For the woman who did everything right—and still feels like something's missing. You were taught that wealth is what you accumulate. Titles. Salaries. Safety. Status. And you built it all. But somewhere along the way, you started disappearing. Maybe you became the strong one. The planner. The provider. The one who made sure everyone else was okay—even when you weren't. You know how to perform. To produce. To prove. But beneath the picture-perfect life, there's a quiet ache: Is this really it?"

Grace's breath caught. She kept reading.

"You're not broken. You're not behind. You've simply outgrown a version of success that was never built for you. Wealth isn't just money. It's choice. It's permission to rest. It's the freedom to stop performing—and start living. It's legacy— not only what you leave behind but how you live now."

The words blurred. She blinked and kept going.

"You don't need to burn it all down. You don't need to have it all figured out. You just need to come home to the woman you were before the world told you who to be. This isn't a pivot. It's a return. Welcome to Rich Like Her. You already belong."

Grace sat back in her chair.

She read the words again twice, looking for the moment where it started to talk to her like she was a child. Or a checkbook.

She couldn't explain it, only that it hit somewhere deeper than words.

It wasn't ambition – she'd had plenty of that.

It wasn't guilt – she'd lived with that, too.

This was quieter. Gentler. A feeling she hadn't recognized in months, maybe years.

Permission.

"You don't need to burn it all down. You don't need to have it all figured out. You just need to come home to the woman you were before the world told you who to be."

She whispered into the stillness, "I can honor him... and still choose me."

She didn't yet know what that meant.

Only that the day that led her here had begun differently.

Before dawn, Whitmore Tower was still. The faint whir of the elevators drifted upward through the building, a sound she'd grown up with—a constant reminder that the Whitmore name never really rested.

In the dark glass, her reflection waited: silk blouse, hair pinned smooth, spine straight. The discipline she'd inherited right alongside the money—the foundation, the expectations, the weight of proving she deserved it.

Grace set her coffee on the desk and woke up her mouse. The screen's pale light rose across her face as she read the words committed to memory long before she'd believed them.

> *"I believe it's time to redefine what the Whitmore Foundation stands for. For decades, we've honored an extraordinary legacy. Now, it's time to build on that foundation—with vision that meets the moment ahead. What our community needs now is relevance, resilience, and reach. Today, I'm introducing the Strategic Renewal Initiative—not as a proposal but as our next chapter."*

She paused on the final phrase. *Our next chapter.*

It sounded steady. Responsible. Exactly what was expected of her.

And yet, for the first time, she wondered if duty could also be a tether—one that bound her to a story she respected, even as it kept her from writing her own.

She let out a slow breath.

His reflection surfaced in the dark glass—her father's face, proud and unblinking, the same expression he'd worn at every board meeting and birthday party alike.

She hadn't realized how much of her life still bent toward his approval.

The door opened softly, and Theresa stepped in, balancing two cups of coffee and a leather-bound folder against her hip.

She'd been with the foundation for nearly thirty-five years—long before it passed to Grace. A lifetime of hearing her father's voice echoing through these same halls, and to still call Grace "honey" when no one else was around.

"You beat me in again," Theresa said, setting the coffee on the desk. "You know the sun doesn't clock in until after 7:00 this time of year?"

She set the folder on the desk and smiled.

"Your dad would've loved seeing you here this early. He always said half the battle was won before the rest of the world woke up."

Grace smiled faintly. "He wasn't wrong. I guess some habits stick."

"Not habits," Theresa said, shaking her head. "Work ethic like that runs in your family."

Grace looked down at her hands. "Yeah," she said quietly. "He never asked for anything he wasn't willing to do himself."

Theresa slid the folder across the desk. "Board packet, your expansion folders and the one-pager. All buttoned up and ready for your magic touch."

Grace didn't reach for it right away. "Let's hold off. I'm not ready to put anything new in front of them yet."

Theresa paused, one brow lifting. "You've been saying that for months."

"I just want to make sure it's right," Grace said. "He built this place from nothing. I don't want to move too fast."

Theresa's voice softened. "Honey, your father built it so it could move. He trusted you for a reason."

Grace smoothed the edge of a page that didn't need straightening. "I know. I just..." She hesitated. "It's easier to keep what he built than risk changing it."

Theresa smiled—patient, knowing. "You sound just like him when he started. Afraid to put his name on the door."

Grace huffed a quiet laugh. "Yeah, well. Maybe the apple didn't fall far."

"Maybe," Theresa said, rising to leave. "But he didn't name you as his successor to keep polishing his apples. He trusted you to plant your own tree."

By midmorning, the boardroom buzzed with muted greetings and the clatter of espresso cups. The Whitmore Foundation's board table gleamed, long-grain walnut framed by floor-to-ceiling windows overlooking the Puget Sound.

Grace stood at the head, presentation slides queued, her notes neat but barely needed. Competence had become her comfort—the one thing she could still count on to make sense.

"This quarter, we're focusing on giving more money to digital-literacy programs, reallocating to strengthen local capacity, and testing partnerships with tech companies that help underrepresented communities."

Her voice was balanced, calm. Almost too calm.

Richard Bainbridge, board chair and her father's longtime confidant, leaned back in his leather chair, fingers steepled.

"Impressive work, Grace. Your father would've been proud. He always believed in long-term bets on tech."

Grace nodded politely. "Thank you. I hope we're continuing in that spirit."

Helen DuMont, the kind of woman who could make a power play sound like a compliment, tilted her head.

"And this new initiative—was that James's idea? Or yours?"

Grace paused, calibrating. "Adjacent ideas were discussed. The framing is mine. I'd like to think it builds on what came before—while looking forward."

Sanjay Patel, pragmatic and allergic to risk, tapped his Montblanc pen against the table.

"Interesting angle. Just tread carefully. Legacy relationships are delicate. We can't jar longtime donors."

Michelle Liu, the youngest board observer, leaned forward, eyes bright.

"But isn't legacy supposed to evolve?" she said. "If we only protect what's already been done, we stop growing. This feels like a way to include people my age—to make the foundation part of what's next, not just what's been."

The room went still.

Richard offered a diplomatic smile. "A fair point, Michelle. And that's why Grace's leadership matters. She represents continuity—the kind that donors trust." He turned toward Grace. "You carry that steadiness well."

Grace smiled reflexively—calm, unreadable. "I appreciate that. Stability is part of our promise."

Helen interjected, gracious but pointed. "Before we wrap, Grace—any areas on that initiative you'd like more input on?"

Grace hesitated. The truth pressed against her throat, small but insistent.

She exhaled. "Honestly? All of them."

A ripple of polite laughter moved around the table. Except Michelle. She didn't laugh. She just watched Grace—steady, curious—as if she'd heard what everyone else missed.

Grace sat straighter than she felt, nodding at something she didn't hear.

But inside, the longing was louder than the polite applause.

For space.

For her own voice.

For the freedom to stop asking, *What would Dad have done?*

When the meeting ended, Grace stayed seated, pen balanced between her fingers, staring at the notes she hadn't written.

Her plan was sound. The numbers were solid. Every metric said the foundation was thriving.

So why didn't she review it with the board?

She gathered her papers slowly, each movement careful, practiced—her father's kind of order.

But the question that had started in Michelle's voice wouldn't quiet.

If legacy was supposed to evolve... how?

The last of the board members drifted out, their voices fading down the hall. Michelle lingered, her chair still turned slightly toward Grace.

When the door finally closed, she stood and crossed the room.

"You know they're not saying no to your ideas, right?" she said softly. "They're just... not sure what you're proposing."

Grace gave a faint smile. "That's generous."

Michelle's lips curved. "You have the packets and one-pager, why not float the idea?"

Grace almost laughed, then caught herself. "Change takes time."

Michelle tilted her head. "Sometimes you just need to see it's possible."

Grace stated to walk towards the door. "It's complicated. Legacy carries weight."

"I get that," Michelle said. "But so does relevance. And you're the only one in that room who can balance both."

Grace looked at her then—really looked. There was no challenge in Michelle's gaze, just quiet conviction.

"I'm not trying to undo what he built," Grace said. "I just don't want to be the one who breaks it."

"Then don't break it," Michelle said. "Build from it."

Grace nodded. Michelle made it sound simple, even easy. It didn't feel that way.

As Michelle turned to leave, she glanced back. "For what it's worth," she said, "they will listen. They just don't know your vision yet."

Grace paused at the door. "Maybe I'm still figuring out which parts of this vision are mine and which ones I inherited from my father."

"Then figure it out fast," Michelle said, tone playful but edged. "Because when you finally speak with your own voice?" She mimed a slow right hook. "They won't know what hit them."

Grace laughed—a real laugh, from her belly, startling herself.

Later that afternoon, sunlight streamed through her office blinds in long golden stripes, catching the edges of her old desk.

Grace sat motionless in the quiet, blazer draped over the chair behind her, meeting notes untouched.

Her eyes lingered on the nameplate: James Whitmore

Her father went by James in Seattle. But his given name was Jae-Min Woo—a name threaded with generations of Korean history and quiet resilience.

He was born in Busan, the eldest son of a scholar and editor, and immigrated to the US at eleven with his mother and younger sister. His father had died just months before they left.

In America, Jae-Min quickly learned that fluency and brilliance didn't shield you from being made small. Teachers mispronounced his name. Classmates mimicked his accent. His questions in class went unanswered.

At seventeen, after landing a prestigious journalism fellowship, a senior editor took him aside and said, "You're smart as hell, but no one's going to remember a name like that."

It wasn't meant as cruelty. More like a whispered code for getting through.

By twenty, Jae-Min Woo had become James Whitmore. The surname was taken from a street near his university—respectable, American, safe.

He told the story with pride and framed it as strategy.

But Grace understood now what her father never said out loud: to belong, he'd had to trade pieces of himself.

Grace grew up with that story in pieces—always told with pride, never regret. Her father had framed it as foresight—a chess play that gave them a better board to play on.

But now, she felt the undertow of what he never said.

A part of him stayed buried in the name he left behind.

A soft knock broke her thoughts. Theresa stepped in, folder still in hand, but she didn't open it.

"Any movement on your proposal?"

Grace didn't look up. "Timing's off. I need to be smart about it."

Theresa softened, voice dipping maternal. "Grace... you'll know when it's time."

She placed the unopened folder gently on the desk, then left without waiting for a response. The door clicked softly behind her.

Grace sat in the quiet. The folder waited on the desk—sealed, heavy, full of things she wasn't ready to face.

So much of her life felt like that lately—unfinished, unresolved, quietly waiting for her to choose.

Before she could overthink it, she dialed her aunt's number.

Her aunt answered on the third ring.

"Grace-ah. I felt your energy shift today. What's going on?"

Grace let out a soft laugh. "Do you always have to be psychic?"

"Always," Eun-Ji replied warmly. "It runs in the bloodline. Now, tell me—did you finally tell that board what you actually think?"

Grace leaned against her desk, the golden hour light now slipping into dusk.

"It went fine. I covered what I was supposed to. Just not what I needed to."

She exhaled slowly. "I had a vision, Auntie. Grounded. Clear. It felt like me. But once I sat down, I just couldn't find the courage to present it."

Eun-Ji laughed softly. "Well, at least you didn't apologize for existing. That's growth."

Grace went quiet for a moment. "Have you ever felt like you were living in someone else's shadow?"

"All the time," Eun-Ji said. "Especially at your age. It's the firstborn daughter curse. We're raised to mirror what we see, not to question what we want."

"But I've been handed everything—respect, reputation, influence. Who am I to question it?"

"You didn't build that foundation, sweetheart. You inherited it. That's not the same thing as owning it."

Grace straightened, walking the length of her office. "Everyone keeps saying how proud Appa would be. But they don't know the pressure."

Eun-Ji's tone softened. "Legacy can feel like a burden, Grace. Or a choice. And if you don't decide what it means for you, someone else will."

Grace's voice dipped into vulnerability. "You make it sound easy. Like you always knew how to break away from expectations."

"I didn't break away," Eun-Ji said. "I got pushed."

Grace stopped walking.

"I told your Appa I was keeping my Korean name," Eun-Ji continued. "He didn't speak to me for two months. Said no one would take a 'Eun-Ji' seriously. That I was making life harder for myself on purpose."

Her voice held steady, but the weight was there.

"I went into law when there were maybe five Asian women in the whole program – and two hundred men. I got passed over for promotions because I spoke up. I turned down jobs that would have looked good in the letters home. And yes, I got labeled— difficult, ambitious, bossy. But I kept going. Not because I was fearless but because I was tired of being a good girl."

The words hit Grace in her chest, heavy and liberating.

"You think you're honoring your father by preserving the mold he left behind," her aunt said gently. "But real honor? Real honor means building beyond it. It means asking, *What are you willing to be misunderstood for?*"

Eun-Ji's voice gave away her smile. "Grace-ah, whose story are you still trying to tell?"

Grace gazed out the windows long after they hung up. The city shifted from gold to cobalt, windows lighting one by one, the pulse of Seattle nightlife rising from below.

She stood still, jaw tight, mind louder than the streets.

The building was nearly empty by the time she left. The drive home felt different tonight. She wasn't just leaving the office; she was moving toward something softer, a place where the weight she carried didn't feel so heavy.

By the time she walked through her front door, the house was dark but not empty. She toed off her Cole Haans—scuffed from the day but comfortable in a way she never admitted out loud— and set down her bag.

In the kitchen, she poured a glass of water and leaned against the counter in the glow of the refrigerator light.

The soft gleam from the living room TV flickered against the walls. Anna was asleep on the couch, hair tousled, glasses askew, an open novel resting on her chest. Grace smiled faintly. Her wife never made it past nine without dozing off.

Grace stood there, just watching her breathe.

Home felt different from the office—not hollow, but warm. Lived in. The kind of space that didn't demand anything from her. No speeches to deliver. No decisions to justify. No weight of being the one everyone looks to.

Through the window, the back garden glowed faintly under the porch light, the raised beds she and Anna had planted last spring now wild with late-summer herbs and stubborn marigolds. The faint scent of rosemary drifted in whenever the wind moved the screen door.

Even the creak of the old floorboards felt grounding here, like the house itself exhaled when she walked in.

Home wasn't for show. It was layered. It was where mismatched rugs and overwatered plants belonged beside heirloom china. Where she could set down her role at the foundation and simply exist as Grace—tired, barefoot, and still figuring it out.

For the first time all day, her shoulders dropped.

What would it feel like if work felt even half this alive? Half this real?

The day replayed itself in shards: Michelle's comments. Eun-Ji's quiet push. The manifesto's whisper: *You already belong.*

Tonight, she wasn't trying to silence the replays. She didn't push the thoughts away this time. She just let them sit there, asking for something different.

In the living room, she draped a blanket over Anna's legs. Anna stirred, mumbling sleepily, "You're home."

Grace bent down, kissed her forehead, and whispered, "Yeah. I'm home."

Anna blinked herself half-awake, a groggy smile softening her face. "What time is it?" She yawned, stretched. "How was work?"

Grace hesitated—her usual "it was fine" balanced on her tongue. But the words never made it out. She sank into the chair besides Anna, eyes on the dark window.

"I read something online today," she said quietly. "It said wealth isn't about money. It's about having room to be yourself. That felt... new."

Anna tilted her head, studying Grace's face. "That sounds... good."

"It was... different," Grace said, a little surprised by how it stayed with her. "I don't know why, but it made me think about Dad—and everything he built. It's incredible, really. I just—" She stopped, searching. "I don't know if it fits me the same way."

Anna reached for her hand. "So, what does?"

Grace stared at her, searching for an answer she didn't fully have yet. But what she felt was undeniable: this—this home, this love, this peace—was the truest thing she knew.

"I don't know yet," Grace admitted softly. "But I think it starts here. Whatever this feeling is... I want to carry it into that building. I want them to feel this."

Anna squeezed her hand. "Then maybe that's the beginning."

Grace exhaled, a low laugh breaking loose.

The weight she'd been carrying didn't vanish. But for the first time, it felt lighter. Not gone, just... shared.

As she climbed the stairs to shower, she glanced once more at Anna curled on the couch. Her safe place. Her proof that she could live differently from the story she'd inherited.

Tonight, the questions felt like permission.

It felt like a beginning.

Performing Perfection

when success becomes the mask
you forget you're wearing

THE HOUSE FELT VACANT, STRIPPED OF THE NOISE THAT ONCE made it home. Elena stepped inside; dim light, cold air. No Mateo. No heavy footsteps. No teenage stomping down the hall. Just the sound of the room breathing, punctuated by the occasional buzz of her phone.

She didn't check. She dropped her clutch on the console—right where it belonged. Unclasped her watch. Headed straight for the bar cart in her living room.

This drink wasn't for celebrating. It was for going numb.

If I can't feel it, it can't touch me.

The first sip burned. Sharp. Familiar. The house stared back. White sofa. Perfect lines. Everything she'd built. Everything empty.

In the mirror above the console, her reflection was elegant. Makeup intact. Blowout perfect. Posture locked.

No one would guess she'd barely held it together in the prep kitchen.

Almost.

She wiped off her lipstick first—always the lipstick. Then the earrings. The diamonds caught the light before hitting the marble.

With some liquid courage, she decided to send an audio text to Seth. She set her glass down and took a deep breath. Her voice was steady, practiced. Casual—but not too casual.

"Hey... wow, it's late. Or early. I don't even know. Just wanted to say thanks again—for earlier. The rooftop. The drinks."

She let out a soft laugh, barely audible.

"I haven't eaten today. Isn't that ridiculous? Like... not even a protein bar. Just champagne and... celebration. Which, shocker— don't keep you full."

She paused, the voice dropped lower, more real now.

"Anyway... I keep replaying everything. What I said. What I didn't say."

Her finger brushed the stop button – then moved past it.

"I wanted to stay longer. With you, I mean. But I panicked. Or... protected myself. Kind of the same thing, right?"

A tight swallow.

"*Dios*, what am I even saying? Don't send this."

Her finger hovered over delete.

But just before she stopped recording, she whispered, "But you made me feel seen."

She sent it before she could stop herself.

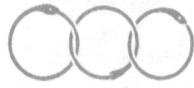

Eight hours earlier, Elena had handed Mateo a smoothie in her Coral Gables home. The air-conditioning fought a losing battle against the Miami humidity; her natural curls forming over her white robe.

"Drink at least half," she said.

Mateo's hair hung in his eyes. He barely touched the glass, frowning.

"It's warm."

Elena pushed the freshly made drink closer. "That's what happens when you let it sit, Mateo. Smoothies don't wait."

Mateo wiped his hands on his ripped jeans. "I didn't ask for this... healthy, liquid, non-breakfast thingy."

Elena shook her head. "And yet... here it is. Call it a love smoothie."

Mateo brushed his bangs out of his eyes. "Mom, you could have just said good morning."

He dipped his finger into the smoothie, licked it, then took a few sips.

"You have that work event tonight, right?"

"Mm-hm," she murmured, turning to make her coffee—café con leche—her one indulgence before the chaos started. "Major client showcase. Everything has to be perfect."

Mateo scooped at the smoothie. "You ever wish you didn't have to go?"

Elena paused, surprised. "Go where?"

"To all your events—open houses, fancy dinners....." He shrugged. "Stay at home for once."

She leaned against the island with her coffee. "Sometimes. But staying here doesn't build a business."

"But didn't you already build it?" Mateo said, looking at her like she was missing something obvious. "Maybe it's not supposed to be so hard?"

Her laugh was soft but weary. "Hard's the job description. You'll get it one day."

"Nope....I don't want your job."

"That's fair," she said evenly. "But you'll want options. And options cost something."

He frowned. "You always say that. You're, like, always in work mode."

Elena hesitated. It landed.

"That's what happens when people rely on you," she said quietly. "You have to show up."

Her phone buzzed on the counter. She ignored it.

Mateo glanced out the window at the palm trees swaying. "Or you ghost."

The word cut. Elena straightened. "Excuse me?"

"Never mind."

"Mateo." She softened her tone. "Look at me."

He turned reluctantly. She touched his shoulder. "I'm doing this for us, *mijo*."

Mateo snorted. "Oh, now I'm *mijo*? You only bust out the Spanish when you feel guilty."

Her voice came out rougher than intended. "Watch your tone."

"Watching," he muttered, arms crossed. "Always am."

Elena exhaled through her nose. "This isn't the time."

"It never is," he fired back.

Silence. The spoon spun in the glass, a metronome to their standoff.

Finally, Elena said softly, "I'll think about that."

The words felt strange in her mouth—less like deflection and more like a confession. It wasn't what she meant to say, but maybe it was what she needed to admit.

Before Mateo could answer, tires crunched on the driveway, followed by the low purr of an engine she knew too well.

Maserati. *Mierda*.

Mateo's face lit up. "Dad's here!" He bolted for the door, smoothie forgotten.

The guard went up. Of course, Derrick was early.

Mateo was already at the door by the time Derrick's Maserati came to a stop. Elena followed, coffee in hand, pulse quickening.

The front door swung open before she reached it.

"Morning, champ," Derrick said, ruffling Mateo's hair. His sunglasses stayed on, smirk dialed up, the faint scent of expensive cologne trailing in.

Mateo grinned wider than he had all week. "Ready for the weekend?"

"Always," Derrick said, tossing a glance over Mateo's shoulder. "Hey, Lena."

The nickname landed like a bruise pressed too hard.

"Derrick," she replied coolly.

And then she heard her: "Oh hiiii, Elena!"

Sierra teetered in behind him, arms full, with a pastel tote and oversized muffins. She was sunshine and effort—everything about her just a little too much.

"I brought homemade banana-chia-flaxseed muffins!" Sierra beamed. "They're vegan and gluten-free."

Elena blinked. "Wow."

"I know how you like to keep in shape," Sierra added brightly.

Elena tilted her head, deadpan. *"Eso es asqueroso."*

Sierra lit up. "Thank you! You're so sweet."

Derrick chuckled low. "Easy, Elena. It's breakfast, not battle."

Mateo was already slipping past them toward the car. "Dad, can we go?"

"One sec." Derrick glanced back at Elena. "Sunday evening?"

"Unless the schedule changes," she replied evenly. "I'll confirm Saturday night."

Sierra stepped forward like she might hug her. Elena shifted back just to make it awkward.

"Oh, and I love your robe," Sierra chirped. "Where's it from?"

Elena glanced down at the white silk draped like armor, then back up with a faint smile.

"Not Zara," she said with a smirk to sting.

Sierra's grin tightened—just a flicker.

Derrick didn't notice. He was already halfway to the car.

Elena leaned against the doorway, arms crossed, watching them go. Mateo didn't look back.

She forced brightness into her tone: "*Te amo*, Mateo!"

He lifted a hand from the back seat, a silent half-wave—eyes still glued to his phone.

The car pulled out. Silence rushed in.

Then—without breaking stride—she dropped Sierra's muffins straight into the trash.

Silence swallowed the house the second the Maserati disappeared down the street.

No footsteps. No teenage groans. The steady pulse of notifications lit up the counter, each one demanding more than she had to give.

Elena stood there to recollect her thoughts, arms crossed, robe still cinched tight like it might hold her together.

Her phone buzzed. She unlocked the screen and pressed the microphone button.

"Confirm lighting grid and press table placement. I don't want any surprises," she said crisply.

She turned and looked around her home. The entrance was grand—arched ceilings, textured stone walls, art chosen to whisper power and taste.

This house was everything she once dreamed of. Bigger than her parents' whole apartment growing up. A long way from that cramped kitchen where she first decided she'd never be poor again.

She had worked hard for this. Fought for every square foot, every detail. The American dream, delivered.

And yet... she stood in the middle of it all and felt nothing.

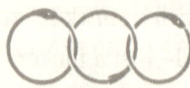

By late afternoon, she was who she needed to be. Beauty was her leverage. She knew it.

The robe was gone. In its place: a crisp white blazer, tailored within an inch of its life, with nothing underneath but bare skin and intention. Lipstick: power red. Louboutin heels: lethal. Hair: smoothed to soft waves that looked effortless but took forty-five minutes.

She didn't need to check the mirror. The pause—and the stares that followed—told her everything she needed to know.

The rooftop bar in Brickell was like a low-voltage current: velvet booths, skyline glittering through glass, music low and lazy—a backdrop for quiet conspiracies.

She exhaled as the elevator doors opened. This was her arena.

"Belvedere and soda with lime," she instructed the bartender without breaking stride.

Conversations thinned as she moved through the bar. Heads turned, eyes tracked. She didn't slow. She didn't need to.

Until she sensed him.

Seth appeared beside her before she heard him approach—casual, the kind of man whose confidence filled the space before he did.

"That penthouse view you staged last month?" he said. "Almost made an offer, and I already own three blocks over."

Elena smirked. "That's the point."

"Making people want what they don't need?" He flagged the bartender. "Dangerous skill."

"Only when it pays."

"And when it doesn't?"

She lifted her glass. "Then it's called flirting."

His laugh was low, easy. "You ever get tired of it?"

"Of what?"

"Playing the game."

Her smile thinned. "I didn't build a career by getting tired."

"Doesn't mean it's not lonely."

She shot him a look. "Says the man who owns three blocks."

"I'm not talking about real estate, Elena."

The shift in his tone made her pause. She looked away first, taking a sip.

"Careful," she said lightly. "I bite."

"Noted." He leaned against the bar.

Her phone buzzed. She glanced down—a text from Mateo.

Hey... can I just stay with Dad this week? Sierra said she'll drive me to practice. It's easier.

Her mask slipped. The rooftop noise blurred.

Seth noticed. "Everything okay?"

She smoothed her expression back into place. "Of course! Teenagers.... twenty words or less."

"Twenty words? That's generous. Mine just grunt."

She smiled, then looked down at her glass. "At least you know where you stand."

He leaned in slightly, voice softer. "Where do you stand, Elena?"

She stared at her empty glass.

"Another drink," she said finally. "And a subject that won't get either of us in trouble."

They traded stories and sideway glances, laughter threading through the noise of the rooftop. For a moment, Elena forgot the armor. She was present, unfiltered, almost safe.

Her phone buzzed.

Derrick.

"Did Mateo tell you he's staying with us this week? Sierra already rearranged her schedule—seems like they've found a good rhythm."

Elena's stomach knotted. Her fingers hanging above the keyboard.

She typed fast: *"Funny. I didn't realize co-parenting meant you and Sierra got final say."*

The reply pinged back almost instantly:

"Clever! But Sierra isn't taking over anything. She's just there. And maybe that's what he needs right now."

Her eyes burned.

The words landed exactly where they hurt most—the place where she secretly worried he was right.

She slipped her phone into her bag, too fast. "I have to run—get ready for my event tonight." Her tone was even, practiced. But her left eye twitched—a micro-tell she couldn't quite control, even when the rest of her face stayed perfect.

"Already?" he said, brows lifting. "Alright. I'll settle up—walk you out, or are we braving the event together?

Another buzz.

Derrick again.

"You're not the only one who wants what's best for him, Elena."

A hollow ache punched through her chest.

Seth noticed as he motioned for the bartender. "What's going on?"

Her eyes flicked up, mask already back in place. "Nothing."

"You sure?"

She exhaled through her nose, steady but sharp.

She didn't look at him right away. Her thumb left a wet streak on the glass.

"That's rich," she muttered finally, "you think I need company."

"Whoa." He leaned in. "What's that supposed to mean?"

Her hand stilled. She set the glass down—careful, deliberate.

"I don't know," she said, voice low. "I'm just stressed."

The word hung there.

Seth tilted his head. "Elena."

She arched a brow. "Yes, *Seth?*"

He nodded, eyes steady.

"I like you," he said simply. "And yeah, maybe you like me. But I'm not going to keep orbiting while you make up your mind."

Silence.

Her lips pressed together. Finally, she said, "So what are you saying?"

Her gaze flicked toward the skyline. Her breath caught.

"I can't risk everything I built for... love," she said at last. "That's not who I am."

"I'm not asking you to risk anything," Seth said. "I'm asking you to let me in."

Something flickered in her eyes. Almost soft. Almost.

She placed her glass on the table.

"I should go," she said, already moving.

Vulnerability wasn't her play. You shift the scene, you move— that's how you keep the upper hand.

Only hours later, the Miami Beach hotel ballroom shimmered under soft amber light– eloquent and entirely hers. Elena had been on-site, micromanaging every detail until her feet started throbbing. Before the first guest could arrive, she slipped away, tucking the day's chaos and every unspoken thing neatly behind her smile. Upstairs, in a quiet private suite, she stripped off her blazer and swapped it for something sharper: a tailored midnight jumpsuit, cut low at the back. Power red lips were wiped clean, replaced with a darker wine shade.

The trick wasn't changing who she was—it was making sure no one ever saw the change happen.

When she stepped back into the ballroom, she felt it—the hush, the half-second pause. Clients, team, friends, all turning toward her just to register her entrance.

This is what she did when it hurt. She controlled the room so she didn't have to feel it.

Polly, in her mid-fifties with a crystal flute in hand, made a beeline toward her.

"Wow, you look stunning! You're like a one-woman empire, Elena. Do you even sleep?"

Elena's laugh rang out, warm, practiced, magnetic. "Sleep? That's tomorrow's problem."

Laughter rippled. Ted, a real estate investor with the confident tan of someone who sailed too often, leaned in.

"If I had half your focus, we'd be retired on a beach in Tahiti by now."

Carmen and her husband joined the circle. Carmen's grin was wide, admiring.

"We were literally just saying—how does she do it? You're basically untouchable."

Elena smiled, moving through them like a current—hugging, clasping hands, pairing investors with influencers in sharp, intentional introductions.

Every detail—the orchids perfuming the air, curated playlists—made this not just a party but proof.

Elena wasn't just the architect. She was the attraction.

Joy, a longtime client with soft eyes and a sharper bob, caught Elena's arm mid-stride.

"How do you keep it all together?"

Elena winked. "Smoke, mirrors, and a 4 a.m. wake-up call."

Joy tilted her head, curious. "Do you ever just... relax?"

Elena's smile held for a beat, then faltered, barely.

"This is me relaxing," she said lightly.

More laughter. More flattery. Elena turned before anyone could see her shoulders drop.

She scanned the room, searching for her next move—then froze.

Seth.

He was across the room, deep in conversation with a blonde in a dress that whispered danger. Beach waves, legs for days, a laugh that floated above the lo-fi jazz.

Elena's gaze lingered longer than it should have. Her chin lifted —automatic, defensive.

What are you doing? Feeling possessive? Seriously?

The thought was sharp, but the ache was sharper.

She exhaled deliberately, adjusted the fall of her jumpsuit, squared her shoulders, and pivoted toward the next VIP.

Her phone vibrated.

Derrick.

"You're not the only one calling the shots, Elena."

The words burned through her like a low-grade fever.

She didn't reply. Instead, she spotted them—her mother in a soft coral dress, her father in the stiff suit he saved for weddings and graduations. They stood out here: proud, slightly awkward, smiling too big.

This night had cost more than their last two years' salary combined.

Her mother reached her first, arms warm and familiar. "*Mija*, have you eaten anything today? You look radiant, but your eyes..."

Elena laughed—soft, brittle. "Mom, it's called intermittent fasting."

Her mother didn't bite, just gave her that look—the one that said, *I see you, even when you don't want to be seen.*

Before the silence could stretch, her father jumped in, pointing across the room.

"You see who's here? William Alcott—founder of Alcott Development. Owns half the skyline between Miami and Dubai. If you can land someone like him, *mi niña*, you'll be on the cover of Forbes Latino next year."

Elena's rolled her shoulders back. She lifted her champagne flute too fast.

"Dad, tonight isn't about poaching whales. It's about celebrating what I've already built."

He laughed, unbothered. "Exactly. So don't slow down now."

Her mother bumped his elbow, a gentle reprimand. "Never mind him. You've already made us so proud. You don't need to prove anything tonight."

Elena's gaze drifted past them, past the skyline, past the crowd. The mask stayed on, but behind it, her eyes ached.

She exhaled, leaned in, and kissed her mother's cheek.

"Thanks, *Mamá*," she murmured. "But as you both know, proving it is the only way they see it. I, uh—put you both at my table, front row," she said. "Go mingle. I've got VIPs to talk numbers with."

Her father beamed. Her mother studied her—quiet, protective. Something was off.

Elena pivoted too quickly, already halfway across the room. But when she glanced back—just once—her mother was still watching.

The breath caught in her throat. Her vision blurred for half a second.

What is happening to me?

She turned away fast. The crowd felt tighter now, the glittering conversation suddenly unbearable.

Heels landing like punctuation, Elena moved swiftly across the rooftop and pushed through the kitchen doors.

The music and laughter muffled behind her. For the first time all night, she was alone.

Her hands were shaking.

The kitchen swayed with its own rhythm—waitstaff threading through swinging doors, silver trays clattering, chefs shouting times. Chaos, but not hers. It was almost soothing.

She exhaled sharply, bracing her palms against cool stainless steel counters.

"Hey, girl." Vanessa's voice came from behind her—warm, steady. A hand landed on Elena's back, one of the few touches she still allowed.

"Congratulations," Vanessa said, eyes scanning her. "This is quite a night and that is quite the outfit! But seriously—how are you really doing?"

Elena crossed her arms as an automatic defense. "What do you mean? I'm fine."

Vanessa arched a brow. "Fine? Girl, you're fine like a house fire with fresh flowers in the windows. We've been best friends since third grade. I can tell when you're barely keeping it together. What's going on?"

Elena let out a dry laugh. "That's poetic. Maybe you should start a podcast."

Vanessa stepped closer, her tone softening. "I'm serious, Ele. You've built something incredible... but you look like you haven't stopped in months."

Elena swayed in her stilettos, rubbing one foot against the

other. "It's called running a business, Vanessa. You should try it sometime—if you can fit it between your 'find yourself' retreats."

Vanessa grinned, unbothered. "Oh, I found myself, babe. Turns out she likes naps and women who throw fancy parties."

Elena smirked despite herself. "Must be nice."

Vanessa tilted her head. "It is. I've got this crew —no drama, no fake nice. Just honesty. You'd like them."

Elena's curiosity flickered, then shut down. "That's cute," she said lightly. "But I'm good. I've got my own thing."

Vanessa studied her for a long moment. "Do you, though? Or do you just like being the one in control?"

The words landed like a pin drop.

Elena looked away. Silence stretched between them until Vanessa's voice came, low and steady.

"You don't have to do it this way," she said. "You don't have to do it alone. Just... think about it."

She reached into her bag and pulled out something small—a deck of cards, wrapped in a gold ribbon. The top card showed a candlelit table surrounded by shadowed silhouettes.

"Here," Vanessa said, casual but knowing. "Humor me."

Elena raised a brow. "What is this? Healing crystals? Tarot?"

"Kind of," Vanessa said. "More for your mindset than your moon sign."

She slid it closer. "Pick a card. First one you touch."

Elena smirked. "And this is supposed to tell me what?"

"Which voice has been running the show," Vanessa said. "The one you don't even realize you're listening to."

Elena sighed. "*En serio*? I don't have time for this, Ness. There's a whole party out there."

Vanessa smiled, that look she'd perfected after years of friendship—the one that said, *you can lie to me, but I still see you.*

"Yeah," she said softly. "I figured that'd be your answer."

She dropped them in Elena's purse.

Elena warily. "What is this really?"

"A mirror," Vanessa said lightly. "Sometimes it's easier to face what's actually driving you when it's right in front of your face."

Elena let out a half laugh. "You always did have a flair for drama."

"And you," Vanessa countered, "always trust reason more than people. Just think about it."

"I'll play your little game later," she said, voice smooth, eyes unreadable.

"I appreciate the kitchen intervention, Ness," she said lightly. "But I've got things to do."

Vanessa smiled, then pulled her in before she could protest. For a moment, Elena let her. The hug broke through the wall—warm, disarming. Like Mateo's used to be, before everything changed.

When they stepped apart, Elena's voice dropped, just for a second. "I'm glad you're here tonight."

Vanessa squeezed her hand. "Always, babe."

Elena nodded, then straightened. Vanessa recognized the shift, that small, quiet click when a woman locks herself back together. At the doorway, Elena paused to smooth her blazer and reapply her smile.

By the time she stepped through the kitchen doors, she was back on. She hadn't said a word to Seth. Her charm was turned all the way up. The laughter came easy, the champagne refills easier.

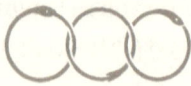

Back at home, the music lingered in her head—low bass, clinking glasses, laughter that already felt miles away.

She took a sip of champagne she didn't remember pouring, the bubbles sharp against her throat.

Then came the fragments, one by one: Sierra's muffins. Derrick's texts. Mateo choosing "easier."

Did they see her waver? Did Seth? Did Vanessa?

Everything she'd built—the empire, the image, the facade—suddenly felt like scaffolding.

And tonight, the cracks showed.

As she passed Mateo's room, Elena stopped. The door was slightly ajar.

The housekeeper—or whatever term people used now—must've come by. The room was pristine—bed made military-tight, desk bare, everything exactly as she liked it.

She pretended it was about order. But really, it was a ritual. A silent way of saying, *I still see you. Even when you're not here.*

Her hand rested on the doorframe. He had asked to stay with them this week. He'd never done that before.

She told herself it was just logistics—Sierra had the flexible schedule; Derrick's house was closer to school. It wasn't personal.

But tonight, that lie didn't land.

In her bedroom, she pulled on her oversized Georgetown hoodie from college—soft, faded, worn from years of chewing the frayed cuffs. It was absurd against the carefully edited wardrobe in her closet, but she wore it to feel the ghost of who she used to be—reckless, broke, naïve enough to believe she could have it all without breaking herself to get it.

She reached into her purse for her phone and felt the corner of Vanessa's little box. Still unopened. Now nudging at her.

The phone stayed quiet. No message from Seth.

Good, she told herself. *Safe. Predictable. Exactly the kind of nothing she could count on.*

Still—his voice lingered. That rare laugh. The way he looked at her, unafraid of the sharp edges.

For a moment, it had felt... good. Unfamiliar.

But she hadn't just been with him. She'd been playing the game—even in those softer moments. Testing boundaries. Flirting like it was a negotiation. Reading every micro-expression, calculating her next move before he made his.

And he knew it. She saw it in his eyes. The flash of exhaustion. The quiet challenge. The *I'm not going to play forever* in his silence.

It should have bothered her less than it did.

Elena knew she pushed people away, knew her armor cut just as much as it protected. But it was like watching a freight train from the inside—hurtling forward, unable to stop, even as she saw the wreck coming.

She wanted to change. Or at least, she thought she did.

She just didn't know where to begin.

The memory sliced through before she could stop it: Derrick's voice, low and careful, saying, *"It didn't mean anything. We were falling apart anyway."* The lipstick on his shirt. The hotel charges she found by accident. The silence when she realized everyone else already knew.

The worst part wasn't the affair. It wasn't even the way he brought Sierra around Mateo before Elena had caught her breath.

It was what came after.

When Derrick blamed her. Told her she'd been too much—too ambitious, too busy, too focused on building something bigger than both of them. That he'd cheated because she wasn't there.

As if her drive, her hunger, her vision—the very things that built the life they lived in—were flaws.

As if wanting more made her unworthy of love.

That was the day she decided softness came with a price. That being *agreeable* for someone else was a game she could never win. That discipline—her walls, her work, her image—her mask—was the only place that still felt safe.

Alone was safer. Alone didn't ask anything of you. Alone couldn't leave.

And yet. The flicker remained—the quiet, traitorous pulse of wanting.

She climbed into bed without ceremony, peeling back the sheets to slip under them. The hoodie bunched awkwardly at her waist, but she didn't care.

The room smelled faintly of her own perfume mixed with laundry detergent—comforting in theory, but somehow still sterile.

Her nightstand told on her: multiple half-empty wine glasses, phone charger dangling off the edge, an old to-do list scrawled on the back of a cocktail napkin.

She built her life around keeping it together. But nights like this? Together fell apart fast.

She kicked off her socks, pulled the blanket up high, and chewed at the frayed cuff of her sleeve—a nervous habit she'd never broken.

And finally... quiet.

For about ten seconds.

Then the replays started. The words she said. The ones she didn't. The ones she'd never admit mattered.

Over and over until they blurred—Mateo's silence, Vanessa's hug, Seth's laugh, Derrick's smirk—a carousel she couldn't step off of.

It was her oldest habit. Her cruelest.

She told herself control was safety. The truth was, control had become the chaos.

Being seen was easy. Staying seen meant performing until she forgot who she really was underneath.

The deeper question hung in the darkness, heavy as the Miami humidity:

How long could you keep building when the foundation was already cracking?

And somewhere in the silence, Elena knew the answer was already coming for her.

The Invisible Cost

what success steals when you stop paying attention

THE HOUSE WAS TOO DAMN QUIET. NO MATEO HOLLERING "MOM, where's my..." from three rooms away, no bass thumping through the ceiling at 7 a.m. because, apparently, fifteen-year-olds had lost the ability to use headphones when focus actually mattered.

Elena stood at the kitchen island with her phone in hand, glaring at the text thread from Derrick like she could will it to say something different.

"If you want to keep him for the week..."

The cursor blinked, waiting. Like everything else in her life lately.

The emptiness felt foreign and familiar at once. As a kid, she'd craved quiet mornings without her mother's rapid-fire Spanish echoing through their cramped apartment, without her father's newspaper crackling like judgment from his chair. As an adult, she'd promised herself a house where she could think, where she could breathe.

Now she had it, and it felt like suffocation.

She should just send the response. Mateo was already settled at his dad's place, probably loving every minute of Sierra's organic smoothie bowls and Pinterest-perfect pantry organization. No shuttling back and forth, no negotiations about homework that wouldn't get done anyway.

Elena had three closings this week and that development proposal she'd been avoiding. A little space might actually be... nice?

But damn, what kind of mother asks for a week off?

The real question, the one that made her jaw lock, was what kind of father got to be the fun parent while she handled the day-to-day? Derrick had walked away from the hard parts of family life and somehow emerged as the hero. Now, Mateo looked at him like he hung the moon, while Elena got eye rolls for caring about dirty clothes on his bedroom floor.

But underneath the friction was something sharper—the memory of her own childhood longings. How many times had she wished her father would just... notice her? Really see her, not just see how clean she kept her room or whether she was being "good."

Elena remembered entering a beauty pageant in middle school. She could still feel the cheap tiara pinching behind her ears, the nylon sash scratching her collarbone. When she hadn't been chosen as the winner, she'd run off the stage, breathless, clutching her 3rd place ribbon like it meant something.

Her father had smelled of aftershave and cigar smoke, his hand heavy on her shoulder as he bent down to say, "Pretty girls always win. Next time, keep your chin up—don't slouch."

That was it. No hug. No "I'm proud of you." Just the lesson, folded into a smile that vanished as he turned to shake another man's hand.

What stayed with her wasn't the applause, or even the ribbon itself. It was the sting of trying to stand taller, chin jutting out the way he wanted, pretending that was enough to make her feel seen.

When had she become the parent who managed Mateo's life instead of connecting with him?

The thought came sharp and uninvited, like a splinter under her skin. She shoved it down with the usual excuses—she was busy, tired, doing her best—but the sting lingered.

Elena took a sip of coffee, grimaced at how cold it had gotten, and set it down harder than necessary. The sound echoed in the empty kitchen.

She imagined herself trying to put words to the ache, then instantly heard Mateo's teenage sarcasm: *"Mom, you're being extra."*

Everything was *extra* these days. The word reduced every effort she'd made to nothing.

For thirteen years, she and Derrick had parented under the same roof. Now, when it mattered most, when a teenage boy needed a father who'd model more than weekend freedom, Derrick had traded curfews and hard conversations for being the fun parent.

No rules. No lectures. Just concert tickets and letting him stay up all night.

Her concern about his grades? Extra. Asking who he was texting at dinner? Extra. Expecting actual sentences instead of grunts? Definitely extra.

The word stung more than it should have. Extra meant caring too much, trying too hard, being too concerned—all the things her own father had never been accused of.

She'd sworn she'd be different. Warmer. More available.

Instead, somewhere along the way, caring had become overseeing, and overseeing had become... this: a son who mistook her concern for control, her love for intrusion.

Fine. Let Derrick deal with the eye rolls and the selective hearing when Mateo is asked to put dishes in the dishwasher.

Maybe a week of "fun dad" would teach Mateo a thing or two about what he had waiting for him at home.

But even as she thought it, a smaller voice whispered: *Or maybe it will teach him he's happier without you.*

She typed, *"He can stay with you,"* then stared at the words a second too long before hitting send.

The bubble turned blue. Elena exhaled like she'd been holding her breath since dawn.

The relief felt wrong, like celebrating something she should be grieving.

But she realized she hadn't had a week to herself in... fifteen years. It seemed like the kind of revelation that deserved a mimosa.

Hours later, Elena found herself sliding into the corner booth at brunch, already knowing how this conversation would go. Jen was predictable that way—the kind of friend who'd validate your worst decisions with a mimosa and call it "self-care."

Safe friends were easier than real ones. They never asked the questions that might actually crack her open.

Elena had learned early that some friends were helpful for sharing her rare thoughts and feelings, while others were kept around to maintain appearances. Jen fell squarely into the second category.

"How's Mateo doing?" Jen asked.

"Mateo's spending the week with his dad," Elena announced. "They've got a good rhythm going. I don't want to disrupt it."

Jen's face lit up like Elena had just announced a promotion.

"That's so mature of you. And honestly? You deserve this time."

Deserve. Elena let the word settle. *I do deserve this.*

Derrick got Sierra's adoring support. Mateo got his father's undivided attention. Elena knew things would be quiet without Mateo, but she pushed away the irritation by telling herself it would be best. She had a "busy week."

Elena had perfected the friends-catching-up routine over the years, sharing only the version that got the nods, the *good for yous.* Life was easier that way. She maintained the image of the resilient divorcée who could close a seven-figure deal, the woman who had it figured out, the friend who never needed anything from anyone.

Exhausting. But it worked.

"Yeah, some me-time is WAY overdue," Elena said, spearing her avocado toast with more force than necessary.

Jen laughed like this was the height of relatability, but Elena caught herself wondering what Vanessa would say.

She remembered their confrontation in the kitchen. She hated it when Vanessa ambushed her like that.

But it was also why she loved her. Vanessa always gave Elena the truth.

Vanessa would probably say poise was another wall, another way to keep people at arm's length without them realizing it.

Elena's white lies came easily. In real estate, it was always about "the sell." Not the sale of the property but selling the vision. The first version of a story her buyers heard usually became their truth. She'd learned to make every word sound intentional, positioned to get the buyer to make an offer.

"Plus, I've got a huge development proposal to finish. You know how it is."

As the words left her mouth, Elena realized she was compensating again. Even here, with harmless Jen and her bottomless mimosas, she couldn't just... be.

Couldn't admit that she'd defaulted to work over time with Mateo, not because she didn't care, but because she didn't know how to be with him anymore without turning into her father—distant, critical.

Jen kept nodding, refilling their glasses, and Elena let the familiar warmth of approval wash over her.

The walk back to her car felt longer than usual, probably because Jen's validation was already wearing off.

That was the problem with surface level connections—they never lasted. Like sugar highs that left you hungrier than before.

Elena sat in the driver's seat, keys in her lap, watching other people's lives through the restaurant windows. A couple sharing pancakes, leaning in like they had secrets worth telling. A family with teenage kids who were actually talking instead of staring at phones.

When had she stopped being curious about people? When had relationships become transactions—what she could get, what she had to give, how to manage the exchange without getting hurt?

Her phone buzzed. A text from her mother: *"Mija, how was your week? Call me when you can."*

Elena stared at the message, fingers lingered above the keyboard, the reply forming and dissolving in her head.

She could call. Her mother would listen, maybe even understand. But understanding required explanation, and explanation required admitting that she didn't have it all figured out.

"Busy week, Mami. Will call soon," she typed before hitting send.

Another deflection, wrapped in the excuse of a busy schedule.

The drive home was quiet except for some pop song about being "unbreakable." Elena wanted to change the Spotify playlist, but she couldn't quite bring herself to do it.

She thought about Mateo's smile yesterday—how he'd looked genuinely happy in ways she couldn't remember seeing when he was with her.

Was she so busy proving she was a "successful" mother that she'd forgotten how to just... be his mom?

Her father ran the house like a lesson in respect—grades, manners, and composure all part of the curriculum. Effort was expected. Emotion was extra credit.

Her mother's smiles—soft, exhausted, edged with pride—were the kind you gave when you were too tired to fight but too proud to quit.

Approval was the family's unspoken currency, and Elena learned to earn it early—straight A's, perfect appearance, the daughter who never needed reminding.

But sitting back at home now, in a kitchen that gleamed with proof of her discipline, she realized the old formulas didn't add up.

The gold stars, the endless striving—none of it translated to peace.

She could read any room, adjust on instinct, and deliver what people expected before they even asked. But somewhere along the way, she'd lost the part of her that didn't need an audience.

The role had become the woman.

On the couch, her phone glowed with Mateo's name. She'd promised herself she'd call—just to talk. Not to check in or fix.

Just to bridge the quiet that had stretched too long between them.

Her finger lingered above the call button, the name on the screen suddenly too heavy to touch.

What would she even say?

How was school? Are you eating vegetables? I miss you.

He'd hear the effort in every word. He always did.

When had love started feeling like a negotiation?

The phone buzzed with a text from him: *"Dad's taking me to get new cleats tomorrow."*

Her first instinct was to respond with logistics: *"What brand are you getting? What about a new mouth guard?"*

All the managing questions that had replaced the connecting ones.

Instead, she typed, *"That's nice, mijo. Have fun."*

She sent it.

Three dots appeared, then disappeared.

"Thanks, Mom."

It wasn't much, but it felt different. Less scripted, more... real.

Elena set the phone down and realized she was crying—not the dramatic kind but the quiet tears that sneak up when you finally stop moving.

She'd spent years trying not to become her father—too blunt, too hard to please—and in doing so, she'd turned into something else entirely.

Not distant, just managing. Not cold, just composed. Not impossible, just unreachable.

The irony stung. In trying to be the kind of parent who never disappointed, she'd forgotten how to simply be there.

Elena stared at her phone, the cursor blinking in the empty message field beneath Seth's name.

Their quick exchange from this morning still lingered on the screen like something unfinished.

"Had a great time. Let's do it again soon."

His reply: A single heart emoji. Warm enough to keep hope alive, vague enough to drive her insane.

Since then, she'd written and erased at least a dozen drafts.

"How was the rest of your night?" Too eager.

"Thinking about you." Too much.

"Dinner sometime?" Too soon.

Delete. Delete. Delete.

The truth pulsed quietly under all that editing: Seth scared her.

Not because of who he was but because of what he might actually want—*her*.

Not the version she showed the world but the woman underneath, the one she'd forgotten how to be.

He asked questions that didn't let her hide behind her usual strategy.

That was the problem.

She set the phone down, screen darkening. Some connections were too dangerous to keep alive—especially when you'd built your life around looking formidable.

Better to let it fade.

But even as she turned away, she could still feel his gaze from that last night. Steady. Like he'd seen something worth knowing.

When was the last time anyone looked at her that way?

When was the last time she'd let them?

The thought pressed too close. She straightened the stack of mail on the counter, grounding herself in the only things that made sense—numbers, deals, things she could leverage.

Later that afternoon, she showed one of her listings to a potential buyer.

"The Mediterranean styling gives it that timeless elegance buyers are craving right now," Elena said, gesturing toward the tiled foyer of the five-million-dollar listing. "And the open concept flows beautifully for entertaining."

Mrs. Davidson nodded, making notes on her phone. "What about the private schools?"

"Excellent. Some of the highest test scores in the state." Elena's voice carried the perfect blend of authority and warmth she'd spent years perfecting. "Your daughter would have access to AP programs, college prep resources, really everything you'd want."

The words came automatically, the same script she'd delivered hundreds of times.

But as they walked through the remodeled rooms, Elena found herself wondering what it would be like to live here. Really live, not just stage and sell.

Would someone's teenager leave dishes in that hand-painted ceramic sink, or would it stay AD-feature ready forever?

"You really seem to understand what families are looking for," Mrs. Davidson said as they finished the tour. "Do you have children?"

Elena's smile stayed perfectly in place. "I do. A fifteen-year-old son, Mateo."

"Oh, how wonderful. Then you know exactly what we're looking for."

Do I? Elena wondered.

She knew how to sell the dream of family life. But was she living it?

"Absolutely," she heard herself say. "I'll send you the comparable sales data tonight, and we can discuss next steps."

The handshake was firm, professional. Another productive showing, another satisfied client.

Elena waited until Mrs. Davidson's car disappeared around the corner before letting her shoulders drop. Families like hers always wanted the same things—open kitchens, good schools, a place to feel they belonged. Elena had most of that. What she didn't have was the belonging part.

In the empty house, surrounded by someone else's idea of perfect family life, she felt more alone than she had all week.

A few days later, on Thursday night, she stayed late at the office. Other people's problems felt easier than her own quiet house.

When she finally got home, she poured wine before she'd even taken off her jacket.

Her phone buzzed as she settled onto the couch. Derrick.

He'd sent a photo of Mateo mid-kick at his soccer game, jersey stretched tight across shoulders that looked broader than she remembered.

She started typing, then stopped. What could she say that wouldn't sound like she was checking up on him from afar.

Finally: 👍

Safe. Neutral.

She zoomed in on the photo before she could stop herself. When had his jaw gotten so sharp? When had he started looking less like her baby and more like... himself?

There was something in his expression she didn't recognize—a confidence that hadn't been there at home.

Was he happier there? Was he more himself when she wasn't around to manage and worry and inadvertently make everything about her own anxiety?

The thought stung more than she expected.

Elena was reviewing contracts when her phone rang. Her mother's picture filled the screen—a candid shot from last Christmas, masa in her hair from making tamales.

Elena almost let it go to voicemail.

Almost.

"*Hola, Mamá.*"

"*Mija!* I was just thinking about you. How are you? How's Mateo?"

The warmth in her mother's voice wrapped around Elena like a hug she didn't realize she'd needed.

For a moment, she considered telling the truth—that Mateo would be staying at his father's for the first time, that she didn't want to fight, just wanted quiet, and that she felt like she was failing at the one job that was supposed to come naturally.

"We're good, *Mamá*. Busy, you know how it is."

"*Ay*, always busy. You work too hard, *mija*."

"I know, *Mamá*. Things will slow down soon."

"And what about you? Are you taking care of yourself? Eating real food, not just those cardboard bars you love?"

"I'm eating." Elena forced a laugh. "In fact, I just had dinner."

True, if you counted the smoothie she'd gulped between reviewing contracts and disclosures.

"Good. And are you seeing anyone? That nice man you mentioned—Seth?"

Elena's grip the edge of her phone. "We're just friends, *Mamá*."

"Friends can become more, *mija*. But you have to let them in. You can't love someone if you're always keeping your guard up."

The words landed like a gentle slap. Her mother always saw straight through her.

"I'm not keeping my guard up," Elena protested, but even as she said it, she knew it was a lie.

"*Está bien, mija.* I just want you to be happy. Really happy, not just successful."

After they hung up, Elena warmed a bath, her mother's words echoing in the silence.

You can't love someone.

She had built so many walls since her divorce that she'd forgotten what it felt like to live without them.

Elena walked to the kitchen, poured another generous glass of wine and glanced at the console table where she had placed Vanessa's card deck.

The box of cards looked ordinary, until you noticed how unapologetically feminine it was.

With Vanessa, it was always about the "women's circles" and "female empowerment" exercises she somehow made sound life-changing.

"*They're not like regular affirmation cards,*" she'd messaged earlier in the week. "*These actually make you think. Some of them are uncomfortable, but that's the point.*"

Elena wasn't ready for uncomfortable questions—least of all from a deck of cards that thought it knew her better than she did.

Trust me, I've got one inner critic too many.

But now, wine-softened and tired of her own thoughts, she found herself curious.

She opened the box, revealing a deck of thick, cream-colored cards with gold edges. The instruction card read, "*Draw one. Sit with the question for as long as it takes to find a real answer, not the easy one.*"

Elena shuffled the deck and pulled a card from the middle:

"*If you slowed down, what truth might catch up to you?*"

She set the card down immediately, as if it had burned her fingers.

"Nope," she said aloud to the empty room. "Not tonight."

But as she put the deck away, the question followed her.

What was she protecting herself from?

The obvious answer was failure, but that felt too simple. She'd failed plenty of times and survived.

Maybe she was protecting herself from stillness. From the questions that rose up when she stopped moving to hear them.

From the possibility that beneath everything she'd built, she was still that thirteen-year-old girl desperate for her father's approval. Still that new mother terrified of damaging the precious life in her care. Still that woman who'd rather live unseen than be seen and left again.

She submerged in a hot bath and tried to let the noise drown out the truth taking shape in the silence. Sleep came late and light, more like a pause than a rest.

Saturday morning arrived without ceremony—no sneakers hitting the floor, no *"Mom, I can't even right now—"* punctuated by the faint music from his headphones, his usual signal that the conversation was over.

The emptiness settled around her, thick and unfamiliar, like the house didn't quite know what to do without him either.

Elena padded into the kitchen in her robe, poured coffee into a mug, and stood there holding it like the warmth might seep into more than just her hands.

Through the window, she watched her neighbor loading beach bags into his SUV, two kids bouncing around him like excited puppies. The dad looked harried but happy, the kind of controlled chaos Elena used to dream of when Mateo was small.

Her neighbor tossed a football to his kids, their laughter carrying across the yard. Elena watched for a moment as they drove off, unsure whether she envied their ease or just missed knowing how to feel it with Mateo.

By midafternoon, Elena had cycled through every distraction in reach. Laundry folded. Groceries ordered. A half-hearted scroll through Instagram that made her want to throw her phone into the sink.

She found herself in Mateo's room without meaning to go there, sitting on the edge of his unmade bed like she was visiting a museum of their shared life.

His old soccer cleats were by the closet, grass stains still visible on the white leather. A stack of books on his nightstand—some for school, others he'd chosen himself.

When had he started reading books on animal physiology?

A photo on his dresser caught her eye—the three of them from two summers ago, arms around each other before a game. All genuinely smiling, not the posed kind but the spontaneous laughter that happened when Derrick made some ridiculous joke about her sunscreen application on Mateo.

Looking at it now, she could see what she'd been too busy to notice then: how he'd started matching her energy instead of bringing his own. How his natural exuberance had dimmed to accommodate her constant state of semi-stress.

The memory came without warning—Mateo at eight, bursting through the front door after school with dirt on his knees and pure excitement radiating from him.

"Mama! Mama! We found a bird's nest at recess, and Mrs. Chen said we could watch the babies hatch, and I want to be a vet when I grow up!"

Elena had been on a work call, phone pressed to her ear, trying to negotiate a difficult contract while stirring dinner with her free hand.

She'd held up one finger—the universal sign for *wait*—and watched his face fall.

"That sounds amazing, *mijo*," she'd said when the call ended, but the moment had passed. His excitement had folded inward, replaced by the polite attention children gave adults who were only half-listening.

How many moments like that had she missed? How many times had she chosen the urgent over the important?

She thought back to last month when Mateo was home sick with the flu, asking if Dad could bring him soup. Not her. Dad.

After she'd been up all night monitoring his fever and rearranged three client meetings to stay home with him.

When he wanted comfort, he asked for Derrick, the man who'd left them both.

Elena wiped her eyes with the back of her hand, surprised to find them wet.

When had she started crying?

The house felt too loud, too full of all the conversations they weren't having, all the connections she'd traded away for what? Prestige? Image?

I'm sorry I've been more of a manager than a mother lately. I'm afraid I'm failing at the most important job I'll ever have. I don't know how to love you without trying to orchestrate everything about your life.

Those were the real conversations waiting to happen. But Elena couldn't imagine speaking them out loud to Mateo, who wasn't just her son anymore but a young man.

They required a vulnerability she'd learned to avoid after the one person who vowed to love her endlessly...

She didn't have time to face the wounds that were still healing.

But it made her wonder: What was Mateo carrying? What was he experiencing?

They never really "talked" about the divorce. It was all matter-of-fact, like one of her listings closing at the escrow company. One thousand signatures and then the final realization that it was done. Over. Final.

She typed, *"Thinking about you, mijo. Hope you're having fun."*

The response came quickly: *"Thanks, Mom. Dad's making your favorite turkey burgers. Wish you were here."*

Elena stared at those four words until they blurred.

"Wish you were here."

Not "wish you were here to manage dinner" or "wish you were here to drive me somewhere."

Just... *here.* Present.

She started to type *"Me too,"* then stopped. She started again: *"Maybe next time"* and deleted that, too.

Finally, she wrote, *"Love you."*

"Love you, too, Mom."

It wasn't the deep conversation she'd been avoiding, but it was real. More real than most of their interactions had been in months.

Elena set the phone down and realized something had shifted—not dramatically, more like a door opening a crack, letting in light to see there was something worth looking at on the other side.

Sunday night rolled in like fog, slow and heavy.

Elena curled up on the couch with the last glass of wine from a bottle she'd opened Friday, legs tucked under a throw blanket that smelled faintly of lavender detergent.

The TV was on—some mindless reality show about people renovating beach houses—but she wasn't really watching.

Her attention kept drifting to her phone, to the stack of work she'd brought home, to the box of cards from Vanessa that seemed to be staring at her from across the room.

The week had been full—showings, client calls, negotiating contracts—but not the kind of full that mattered.

It was the kind of busy that kept her moving to avoid the hard questions, the uncomfortable truths, the conversations she wasn't ready to have.

But sitting here now, after a week alone, Elena couldn't ignore what had become increasingly clear:

She was lonely.

Not the dramatic, obvious kind of loneliness that demanded immediate attention, but the subtle kind that crept in around the edges, that made her reach for her phone even when no one was texting.

The text thread with Mateo showed their brief exchange from yesterday, ending with *"Love you, too, Mom."*

Such simple words, but they'd felt like a small miracle when she'd received them.

Maybe that was enough for tonight. Maybe she didn't need to solve everything, answer every difficult question, or transform into someone completely different.

Maybe it was time to notice that something needed to change, even if she wasn't ready to name what that something was.

But as she scrolled mindlessly through her favorite influencers' feeds— tropical getaways, dinner snapshots, families doing family things—Elena couldn't shake the feeling that time was slipping away.

That while she was busy keeping everything running, other women seemed to know the secret—how to work, love, and live without burning out in the middle.

The thought should have motivated her to action—to call Mateo for real, to text Seth, to open those cards and face whatever questions they held.

Instead, she turned on the beach house show, where other people's makeovers were simple, contained and fixable in under an hour.

She'd opened a door earlier, just a crack, when she'd texted with Mateo.

That felt like enough progress for her.

The bigger conversations, the deeper questions—those could wait.

Couldn't they?

Elena finished her wine and let herself sink deeper into the couch cushions, but the questions followed her:

"If you slowed down, what truth might catch up to you?"

The cards sat silent on the console table, patient, holding space for whenever she was ready to stop running.

But not tonight.

Tonight was for the comfort of postponement, for not quite looking too closely at what might be found in the mirror.

By the time the next episode started, Elena had almost convinced herself she'd forgotten what the questions were.

But they lingered in the spaces between thoughts, waiting for a moment when she'd be brave—or tired enough—to finally answer them.

The week ahead stretched before her—routines to keep her moving, achievements to make her feel useful, and just enough productivity to drown out the harder questions about who she was when no one was watching.

For now, adequacy felt like relief.

The Cost of Compliance

what you lose when you play by their rules

THE EMAIL ARRIVED AT 6:47 A.M. WITH NO SUBJECT LINE AND TWO words in the body: *"Emergency All-Hands Meeting."*

Ava stared at her phone screen, coffee mug halfway to her lips. In eight years, she'd never received an email from corporate communications at 6:47 a.m. Ever.

Her phone buzzed immediately. Claire.

"You see it?" No greeting, no morning pleasantries. Claire's voice had an edge Ava had never heard before.

"Just got it. What do you know?"

"Nothing good. Emily from HR called in sick yesterday, except I saw her badge swipe at 11 p.m." Claire's breathing was shallow. "Mike's been in back-to-back meetings since Tuesday. David's been dodging calls. And the executive floor? Dead quiet."

The coffee turned sour in Ava's mouth. "When's the meeting?"

"Nine a.m. From the top of the house. Mandatory."

Ava set down her mug. Mandatory was code for either acquisition or bloodbath, and acquisitions didn't happen at emergency meetings with less than three hours' notice.

"I'm on my way." she said.

"Ava? This actually scares me."

The line went quiet. In eight years, Claire had handled hostile takeovers, market crashes, and a sexual harassment scandal without blinking. Claire didn't get scared.

"Me too," Ava admitted.

By 7:15 a.m., the trading floor sounded wrong. Too quiet, like someone had turned down the volume on people pretending everything was normal. Conversations stopped mid-sentence when she walked by. The usual pre-market energy—phones ringing, keyboards clicking, the smell of people making money— had been replaced by something that felt like a funeral home.

Ava passed the coffee station where three analysts clustered around their phones, voices low.

"... heard it's 15 percent..."

"... my mortgage payment alone..."

"... should've seen this coming when they froze hiring..."

She couldn't breathe deep enough. Fifteen percent was bad. But rumors always started low.

Claire was at her desk with two phones pressed to her ears, taking notes in the shorthand only she understood. She held up one finger—the universal sign for "this is bad, and I'm trying to fix it."

Ava closed her office door and opened her laptop. Seventeen emails since midnight, but nothing from leadership. The absence of information felt louder than any announcement.

Her phone buzzed. A text from David: *"You hear anything?"*

She typed back: *"About what?"*

Three dots appeared, disappeared, then appeared again. Finally: *"Nothing. Never mind."*

She bit the side of her cheek. David didn't text about nothing.

At exactly 8:55 a.m., her calendar notification pinged: *"Reminder: All-Hands. Conference Room A. Mandatory atten-dance."*

Claire appeared in her doorway, face pale. "It's about to start."

"I know." Ava saved her work and closed her laptop. Her hands were steady, but her heart was doing something arrhythmic against her ribs. "How bad do you think this is?"

"On a scale of one to ten?" Claire's voice was barely above a whisper. "Fifteen."

Conference room A was standing room only, which should have felt energizing but no one looked thrilled to be there. The air felt tight, nervous. Ava found a spot near the back. David sat in the front row, his expression unreadable. She tried to catch his eye, but his gaze stayed fixed on the presentation screen.

The CEO—a man Ava had spoken to exactly four times in ten years—cleared his throat. "I'll get straight to it. Market conditions, regulatory pressures, and strategic realignment require us to make some difficult decisions about our workforce structure."

Workforce structure. Corporate speak for "people are about to lose their jobs."

"Effective immediately, we're implementing a reduction in workforce affecting 30 percent of our current staff."

Thirty percent. The rumors were wrong by half. Ava's mind did the math automatically: roughly two hundred people. Two hundred careers, mortgages, families impacted.

"Individual meetings will be scheduled throughout the day. HR will be reaching out directly."

The room was so quiet she could hear the ventilation system. Someone near the front was breathing too fast.

"Questions?"

No one moved. No one spoke. The silence stretched until it became unbearable, and then the CEO nodded. "That's all. Please return to your desks and wait for further instructions."

The exodus was surreal—people filing out like they were leaving a movie theater, except the movie was about their own financial security, and no one knew how it ended.

Back at her desk, Ava stared at her computer screen without seeing it. Her brain kept looping back to that phrase: *30 percent.*

Claire hovered nearby, pretending to organize files. "Your portfolio numbers are solid," she said quietly. "Q3 performance was stellar. The Henderson account alone—"

"Claire." Ava's voice sounded strange in her own ears. "Do you really think we're on the list?"

The pause lasted three seconds too long. "I don't know," Claire admitted. "And that's what's unsettling."

For the first time in her career, Ava didn't know either. She'd always been able to read the room, predict the outcomes, position herself on the winning side. But sitting here, waiting for HR to call, she realized she'd been playing a game where the rules could change without notice—and she'd never actually learned how to play anything else.

Her phone buzzed. Unknown number.

"Ava? It's Sophia Duval. I heard what happened this morning— my friend was in a meeting at Morrison Kline. I've been wanting to call you since our conversation, and when I heard the news... I had to check in."

Ava looked around the office, at people staring at their phones like they were waiting for execution orders. "It's not a great time, Sophia,"

"I know. Word's already making the rounds." Sophia's voice was gentle but direct. "Which means by lunch, every headhunter in the city will know your firm is bleeding talent."

Ava's stomach dropped.

"I know you're probably in crisis mode right now, but can I ask you something? If you found out today you were losing your job, what would you do?"

Ava snorted. "Find another one. What else?"

"Yeah, that's what I said too." Sophia's voice dipped, conspiratorial. "But then I kept thinking... was I just signing up for more of the same? More late nights, more panic attacks, just in a different building?"

Ava didn't answer. She couldn't.

Sophia softened. "Look, I'm not saying that's even on the table right now. But maybe, when you've got a minute, ask yourself a different question. Not *what's next* but *what else could there be?*"

Ava closed her eyes. "I don't have time for philosophical discussions right now."

"Fair. But when you do have time—whether that's tonight or this weekend or after you figure out what's happening with work—I want you to try something. I'll forward it to your personal email."

A pause. Then Sophia's voice dropped lower. "Ava? The same thing happened to me. That's why I left."

Ava started to piece it together. Sophia had left on a Friday. Ava remembered walking in early to catch up on a client proposal marked urgent—meaning someone had sat on it all week and dumped it on her desk. Sophia had been clearing out her desk.

"It's been great working with you," Sophia had said, pulling her into a quick hug. "Take care of yourself, okay? Don't get caught up in all of it."

No drawn-out goodbyes. No hint of where she was headed. Looking back now, Ava realized how Sophia was just gone. She didn't hear a word about her until nearly three months later, when a LinkedIn update announced she'd started at Brown & Stein as a junior partner.

At the time, Ava assumed it was a noncompete.

Now she wondered about the full story.

Despite the scenarios running through her head, Ava kept listening. The truth was, she didn't have a plan. Sure, she'd toyed with fantasies of working from Bali, but if she had to act today, she wouldn't even know who to call. No list of contacts. No safety net.

For the first time, it hit her that Sophia might be her only professional lifeline.

"Ava, don't do this at work. Find a space that's not your office. Get a piece of paper or use your phone. I'll email this over too, but complete this prompt as many times as you can: *'If I could be honest...'* Don't edit yourself. Dream bigger than you've ever allowed yourself to dream. Then ask yourself what it would cost to stay exactly where you are."

The line went quiet except for Sophia's breathing.

"Got it. Hey, Sophia? Thanks for calling. It means a lot."

"I'm here if you need to talk, okay? Reach out anytime."

At 9:47 a.m., HR called.

"Ava? This is Emily from Human Resources. Could you come down to conference room C at your earliest convenience?"

At your earliest convenience. Corporate speak for "now."

Conference room C was smaller, more intimate. Emily sat across from her at a mahogany table with a manila folder, her expression professionally sympathetic.

"Please, sit." Emily opened the folder. "I want to start by saying that your performance has been exemplary. Your portfolio returns, client communication, and leadership contributions haven't gone unnoticed."

Ava's heart hammered, waiting for the "but."

"However, the current restructuring requires us to make some strategic adjustments to team composition and reporting structures."

Here it comes.

"Your position, as currently structured, is being eliminated."

The words dropped like a gavel. Final. Nonnegotiable.

Ten years. Stellar performance. Eliminated.

"Not to worry," Emily chirped, her smile just a little too bright. "We're offering you a role in our client services division. Different responsibilities, with an adjusted compensation package." She slid the manila folder across the table.

"You'd be supporting the relationship management team by directing strategy and operations rather than working in a client-facing role. It's a chance to round out your experience for future advancement."

Ava's stomach dropped. *Supporting. Rounding out.* Downgrades dressed up as opportunity.

Ava studied the numbers. No pay cut, but no equity. A title that sounded impressive but meant nothing. A sideways move presented like a gift.

"I need to think about it," she heard herself say.

"Of course. Feel free to take the rest of the day. We'll finalize everything before Friday of next week." Emily beamed. "We're excited to have you take on this new role—we knew you'd be the perfect fit."

The cheer in her voice landed like a blow.

Ava gathered the folder with steady hands, the kind of steadiness that came only from years of practice. The air in the

conference room felt thin, her pulse still catching on that word—
eliminated.

By the time she reached her office, she was in a daze. Claire
looked up expectantly, but Ava just shook her head and closed
her door.

She grabbed her bag and laptop without explanation.

"Claire, I'm working from home for the rest of the day."

Claire's eyes looked panicked, but she knew better than to ask.

"Cancel my meetings. Forward calls to voicemail. Tell any clients who call that I'm out sick."

She didn't wait for Claire's response. The second she turned
away, the composure cracked, her stride lengthening into something just short of a run. The folder felt hot in her bag, like she
was walking the hall branded with a scarlet D for *demoted.*

The elevator was just ahead. Almost there.

David stepped in just as the doors started to close.

"Ava..." His voice had that careful tone people used when they
were about to deliver bad news they'd already rehearsed. "Look, I
wanted to catch you before..."

"Before what, David?"

His eyes flicked to the grip on her bag, and that was all it took.
He knew. Of course he knew.

The senior leaders probably got the call yesterday, while she
had still been grinding out portfolio proposals.

And then another, sharper thought: *the client dinner with
Tom Henderson. Did he know then, too?*

"They asked me to help with transition planning," he said, like
it was an apology. "The client services role—you'll be great at it.
Michelle's team really needs someone with your skills."

Michelle. Hired two years after her. Sailed to senior director
while Ava kept grinding for the SVP track.

Client services was where careers went to die, and David knew it.

She swallowed hard. When she finally spoke, her voice could have cut glass. "Right. Michelle. The rising star." She didn't spit the words, but they landed like it.

"Ava, come on. You know how this works. It's just business."

The elevator dinged. Ground floor.

"David?" She stepped out and turned back to face him. "Next time you want to deliver bad news you already know, maybe don't ambush someone in an elevator."

She walked away before he could respond.

Ava decided to walk home. She needed air. Space.

It'd been years since she'd taken the long way anywhere—minutes were always more productive in the back seat of an Uber, firing off emails while someone else navigated traffic.

The adrenaline started to wear off around 42nd Street, and the gravity of the situation sank in like cold water.

What would she tell her mom?

Her father's voice came back easily, the one that lived somewhere between pride and pressure:

"No excuses, Ava. You either deliver, or you don't. Winners find a way."

He never said it unkindly. Just as if it were fact.

But what he'd never understand was what happened when the game itself was rigged—when doing everything right still left you invisible.

She'd learned the only way she could: by playing harder. Louder. Sharper. Until she forgot what her own way even sounded like.

She found an empty bench in Bryant Park and sat down hard. The packet inside her bag jammed into her hip, sharp and insistent, like a reminder she couldn't shake off.

For a long moment, she didn't move. Then the world around her edged into focus: dogs tugging at leashes, a man unwrapping a sandwich, a woman turning the last page of a paperback in the sun. People with whole days stretched out in front of them.

What do these people do that they can sit here on a Friday morning? When did I stop noticing that life happens outside of conference calls?

Her phone buzzed. She pulled it from her bag and opened Sophia's email.

The instructions were simple: *"If I Could Be Honest List. Find a quiet space and a blank page (or your Notes app). Give yourself ten minutes and finish this sentence as many times as you can: 'If I could be honest...' Don't worry about whether it's practical. Let what's true rise to the surface. See what surprises you."*

Ava glanced around the park. A businessman strode past, phone pressed to his ear, voice clipped and urgent. He looked exactly like she had only yesterday.

To him, she probably looked unemployed, killing time on a park bench.

It irritated her. It unsettled her.

She pulled out her phone, opened her Notes app, and set a timer.

The screen stayed blank. Nothing came.

She watched a group of women her age, unrolling mats for yoga on the lawn.

She started typing: *"If I could be honest... I want to try yoga. I want to leave early on Fridays."*

She stopped, shook her head. *This is ridiculous. I just found out my job was eliminated, and I'm thinking about yoga?*

But her fingers kept moving:

"*I want to matter. I want my work to mean something beyond making money for people who already have money. I want to build something that outlasts quarterly reports. I want Emma to be proud of me for reasons that have nothing to do with my salary. I want to start living. I want to travel somewhere that isn't a client meeting. I want to fall in love with someone who actually sees me. I want to stop being afraid that if I'm not solving problems, I'm nothing.*"

The words poured out faster than she could think them through, a flood of wants she'd buried under years of keeping her head down and calling it ambition.

"This is ridiculous," she muttered again.

But her fingers kept moving anyway, as if her heart had decided before her head could catch up.

"*I want to work where I want, when I want, with people I like. I want to teach Emma about money without teaching her to be afraid of it. I want to stop equating my worth with my net worth.*"

She paused on the last line.

When did those two things become so entangled that I couldn't separate them?

By the time she left the park, the questions hadn't eased. They sat in her chest like a weight she carried up the steps to her apartment door.

That afternoon, Ava sat in her apartment with takeout containers and a bottle of wine she'd been saving for a special occasion.

The *If I Could Be Honest List* glowed on her phone screen, but the words felt hollow now, like dreams written in a language she'd forgotten how to speak.

She stared at the last line: *"I want to stop equating my worth with my net worth."*

The question pulled at something buried deep, and suddenly, she was twelve years old again, standing in her family's kitchen doorway. Her father sat at the table, with bills spread out like evidence of failure. Her mother hovered nearby, dish towel twisted in her hands.

"We don't discuss money outside this house," he'd said, voice sharp with shame. "And we don't have problems. Just temporary challenges."

But Ava had seen the stack of red notices. The way her mother's face went gray at the mailbox. Even now, the sound of a phone ringing made her stomach clench—like it was still a collector on the other end, demanding what they didn't have.

She remembered walking into that same kitchen with her report card, straight A's across the page. Her father's face had transformed, the tension melting into something that looked like relief.

"Now that's what I'm talking about," he'd said, holding the paper up like salvation. "This is how you solve problems, Ava. Excellence. Results. You keep this up and you'll never have to worry about..." He'd gestured at the bills without looking at them.

Her father had always made it clear that a good education would take her beyond the boundaries of their financial stress.

What stuck was simple: *Perform, and you're secure. Achieve, and maybe, just maybe, you'll be worthy.*

Now, looking back she could see how perfectly she'd internalized the lesson; overdelivering at work, saying yes to every request, tolerating condescension and invisibility because pushing back felt like risking everything.

She'd been seeking approval her entire life.

She opened her voice memo app and pressed record.

"So, I'm disposable. Ten years, all-in. But today, I found out I'm not indispensable. Their big offer? A spot in the client services graveyard. But hey, it comes with benefits!" She took a sip of wine and stared at the takeout boxes on the counter.

"The scary part isn't losing the job. It's realizing ten years of winning bought me nothing I actually wanted."

She glanced at the list on her screen, at the wants she'd never really allowed herself to voice.

"I made a list today. What I really want. Not the checklist crap. Actual wants. And looking at it now, I can see I've been playing it safe. Playing by someone else's rules. And it's already cost me more than I want to admit."

She stopped the recording and listened to the playback. She heard herself clearly for the first time.

If she left it here, it would just sit in her phone with a hundred other notes she'd never revisit.

She needed to see it. Pin it down.

She flipped open her laptop and pulled up the email Sophia had sent. The next question waited on the screen the cursor blinking, impatient.

She typed out the heading: *"The Cost of Staying Stuck."*

At the top, she typed the question:

"What has playing by someone else's rules already cost you?"

The answers came faster than she expected:

"The promotion I didn't get. The clients who smile at the men and skim past me. The relationships I let fade because I was always 'too busy.' The business ideas I shoved into a drawer. The raise I should have asked for by now. The influence I thought I'd have by this point. The life I keep promising myself I'd start once I finally 'arrived.'"

Her brain then defaulted to actual math—numbers were safer than feelings. Missed promotions. Bonuses that never came. Equity she should've had by now. The total in her head was staggering. Millions, maybe more.

But no spreadsheet could calculate the other losses: the years she couldn't get back, the chances she never took, the life she'd been too busy to live.

She glanced at the document, then at the city spread out below her.

For the first time ever, she felt like she might have choices of her own to make.

She sat back, staring at the blinking cursor like it might tell her what came next.

It didn't.

Her phone did—her mom's name lit the screen. Ava stared at it for a long moment before finally answering.

It was 8:30 p.m.—late enough that her mom would worry, but early enough that Ava couldn't justify ignoring it.

"Ava, love! You answered! What a nice surprise. How was your day, sweetheart?"

The cheerfulness made Ava's heart thump. She pressed her palm against her thigh, stalling.

"It was... a lot. I don't really know how to say this, but—" She exhaled. "Mom, I need to tell you something. There were layoffs at work today."

Silence, then, "Oh, honey. Are you okay? Did you... Are you still...?"

"They offered me a different position. Lower level, different responsibilities."

Big sigh of relief. "Well, that's good news then! At least you still have a job. In this economy, you can't be too picky—"

"Mom, it's a demotion. Client management instead of client-facing. No equity upside. It's usually where they move people before they push them out entirely."

Another pause, longer this time. When her mother spoke again, her voice had shifted into crisis mode—the same tone she'd used during the bill-paying kitchen scenes of Ava's childhood.

"Your mortgage... Your car... Ava, do you even have enough savings? What if you can't find another job? What if you get sick? You can't just walk away. Not now. What if—"

"Mom—"

The panic in her mother's voice sparked something primal in Ava's nervous system. Her heart rate spiked. Suddenly, numbers flooded her mind like red alarms: her savings balance, her investment accounts, the gap between what she had and what it would take to feel safe.

"I have to go, Mom. I'll call you tomorrow."

"Ava, promise me you won't do anything rash. Promise me you'll take that job."

Her stomach flipped. She couldn't choke out the one word her mom wanted.

"We'll talk tomorrow. I'm just... tired. I love you."

She hung up before her resolve could break.

The apartment felt smaller now, silence pressing in on her ears. Her mother's questions looped back like sirens: *What if you can't find another job? What if something happens? What if you risk everything?*

Each one hit low in her gut, sharp and unrelenting, until she couldn't tell if the pounding in her chest was fear or anger.

She reached for her phone to record another voice memo, then stopped.

What if her mother was right? What if walking away from security was the same mistake her family spent years recovering from?

The doubt tasted metallic in her mouth, sharp and familiar—the same taste she'd had at twelve, standing in the doorway of her parents' kitchen, watching bills pile up like proof of failure.

She'd made a promise to herself back then: *Not me, not my life. I'll work harder. Run faster. Never let what happened to them happen to me.*

And it worked. Until it didn't.

She turned to the window but only saw her own reflection staring back.

She'd built her whole life on one rule: if she worked hard, she'd be safe. If she achieved enough, she'd finally matter.

Only now, stripped of the title that once defined her, she could feel the truth pressing in.

The rules hadn't saved her. They'd left her here—exposed, replaceable, alone.

Ava sat with that truth for a long moment.

Then she opened her laptop again.

The document was still there: *"The Cost of Staying Stuck."*

She scrolled past the list of what playing by someone else's rules had already cost her.

And then, before she could talk herself out of it, she looked at the next prompt from the email:

"What I'm No Longer Willing to Pay."

Her fingers hovered over the keyboard.
Then they moved.

"I'm not willing to spend another ten years invisible in rooms I set the table for."

"I'm not willing to miss Emma's milestones for clients who forget my name."

"I'm not willing to trade my life for approval that never comes."

"I'm not willing to keep equating my worth with my net worth."

"I'm not willing to stay small to make other people comfortable."

She stopped. Read it back. Felt something shift. It wasn't a decision. Not final. But it was a line in the sand. And for the first time all day, it felt like *her voice.* She saved the document and closed the laptop. Monday, she'd still have to answer Emily. She'd still have to face the choice: take the demotion or walk away. But tonight, she'd done something different. She'd stopped defending the system that erased her. And she'd started naming what she wouldn't accept anymore. It was a small act. But it was hers. And that was a step forward for now.

Stewardship, Not Preservation

*when legacy shifts from
inheritance to intention*

GRACE STARED AT THE CHECK IN HER HAND: SIX FIGURES, MADE out to the Seattle Arts Coalition. The ink was dry. Her signature was perfectly legible. All she had to do was walk twenty feet to Theresa's desk and say, "Please process this."

Instead, she'd been standing in her office doorway for three minutes, paralyzed.

Coffee steamed untouched on her desk. Her calendar blinked with back-to-back meetings. The paper felt heavier than it should.

Their money, she corrected herself. The foundation's money for her to allocate. Money that was meant to be used.

So why did every expenditure feel like theft?

The Seattle Arts Coalition had been her idea. Seven months of research, two site visits, countless hours reviewing their proposal. On paper, it was perfect—aligned with the foundation's mission, impactful, sustainable. The kind of forward-thinking initiative that would create a new direction.

But standing here, check in hand, all she could hear was a voice from twenty years ago:

"Grace-ah, money is not a toy. Every dollar we don't need to spend is a dollar we can give to someone who needs it more."

And underneath that familiar guidance, there was a newer, sharper absence: the silence where his counsel used to be.

What would he think about this decision?

She'd never know for sure, so she played it safe—still trying to please the ghost of his expectations.

Her mind drifted to a memory. She'd been ten, asking for riding lessons like her classmates. The answer had been gentle but firm: horses were expensive, and expensive meant frivolous, and frivolous meant forgetting where they came from.

She'd gotten the lessons eventually—after writing a three-page essay on why equestrian skills would make her a more well-rounded leader and handing it in like a school paper.

Even then, he'd negotiated down to group lessons at a county stable instead of the private academy her friends attended.

Necessary. Responsible. Practical. Those were the rules he lived by.

Now, at fifty-three and running a fifty-million-dollar foundation, she still felt like she was writing essays to justify every decision.

Grace walked back to her desk and deliberately placed the check down so that it covered half of her father's nameplate.

The small gesture landed differently—not defiant, just... proactive.

She touched the edge of the celadon vase—the one constant in this office that predated her title and the transition. The ceramic was smooth under her fingertips, but if you looked closely, you could see the hair-thin lines of gold threading through tiny cracks. She'd once read that celadon symbolized calm and refinement—qualities she'd built her life around.

Kintsugi, her father had called the art technique. A donor from Tokyo had given it to him years ago, explaining that in Japanese art, broken things weren't hidden or discarded—they were mended with gold, made more beautiful because of where they'd been broken.

"Brokenness doesn't diminish value," her father would say. *"It just shows you where the light can shine through."*

Her mother had been the one to place it on his desk. "Something beautiful," she'd said. "So you don't forget—success isn't much good if it isn't surrounded by a little grace."

Then she'd looked at her daughter, smile soft but certain. "You'll understand that someday."

Grace had been twenty-four when her mother died. Too young to understand what she'd meant. Old enough to spend the rest of her life trying to figure it out.

She traced the gold seams again, realizing this was why she had said yes to the Seattle Arts Coalition. It wasn't just about preserving art; it was about honoring the cracks—the resilience, the beauty that could be mended and made whole again.

Twenty minutes later, Grace stood in the foundation's main conference room, leading the quarterly board review with a methodical rhythm. Charts and graphs filled the wall-mounted screens. Board members nodded approvingly at efficiency metrics and impact assessments.

"Our digital equity initiative has reached three thousand students across fourteen districts," she said. "Participation is up twelve percent over projections, with stronger engagement in under-resourced schools."

Richard Bainbridge leaned back in his chair, fingers steepled. "Impressive work, Grace. Your father would be—"

"Proud, yes." Grace's interruption was smoother than silk, but the repetition felt like scratching a record. "The real credit goes to our community partners. They're doing the work that matters."

Helen DuMont adjusted her pearls—a tell Grace had learned to read. It meant unease, which showed itself in the edge of her voice.

"Speaking of community investment, where do we stand on the arts coalition funding request? I believe we tabled that last quarter."

Grace's pulse quickened. The check was still sitting on her desk unprocessed.

"We're... conducting final due diligence. I want to ensure full alignment with our strategic priorities."

Translation: I'm scared to send it.

Sanjay Patel, the board's human metronome, tapped his pen—another tell. Impatience disguised as thoughtfulness.

"These cultural initiatives are important, but we need to be careful about mission creep. Arts funding is a nice-to-have, not a need-to-have."

Michelle Liu, now officially on the board, looked up from her notes.

"Actually, Sanjay, the data tells a different story. Communities with strong arts programs show measurable improvements in education, mental health, and economic development. This isn't separate from our mission—it's foundational to it."

Grace paused.

Michelle had done the homework Grace wished she'd had the courage to share.

"Interesting point," Richard said diplomatically. "But we're stewards of significant resources. Caution is... appropriate."

There was that word again. *Appropriate.* The word that had shaped her entire life.

Grace nodded, the good daughter in the boardroom. "Of course. I'll have a recommendation by next quarter."

The word settled in her chest like a stone. She'd been hearing it her entire life—the golden rule that had kept her safe, successful, and increasingly smaller.

But as the meeting progressed, she couldn't shake Michelle's words: *It's foundational to our mission.*

Not frivolous. Not nice-to-have. *Foundational.*

When had she forgotten the difference?

After the meeting, Grace retreated to her office to find Theresa organizing a stack of invitations on her desk.

"Galas, grant ceremonies, the usual suspects," Theresa said without looking up. "But this one's different."

She held up an elegant cardstock invitation.

Grace took it—heavy paper, elegant typography, but warmer than the typical formality:

Whole Woman Wealth: A Reflection Circle

An intimate virtual gathering for women who've built extraordinary lives—and want to make sure the way they're living still reflects what matters most.

Saturday, 10 a.m. – 1 p.m.
Private virtual gathering
Limited to eight participants

Grace turned the card over. On the back, written in fountain pen ink:

"Grace—Your impact at the foundation precedes you. This gathering is simply a space to pause, reflect, and ask what else might be possible. No obligations. Just curiosity. — Kate"

Grace held the invitation longer than she meant to, noticing how different it felt from the usual gala invitations—less production, more... personal. Like someone had actually thought about what she might need instead of what she could provide.

"Have you seen this before?" Grace asked.

Theresa glanced at it. "Kate called yesterday while you were in meetings. She said Michelle Liu recommended you—mentioned she'd seen someone carrying more than she needed to."

Theresa paused. "Kate seemed genuine—not pushy, just... really engaged. She asked for your best address and said if it wasn't meant for you, you'd know."

Theresa's voice softened. "Honestly? I liked her. Didn't sound like the usual pitch."

Grace set the invitation down but didn't push it away. "That's not my world. I don't sit in circles talking with strangers about... who knows what."

"Why not?" Theresa's eyebrow arched. "Maybe it's just a chance to sit with women who understand what it means to always be *on*."

Grace's head snapped up. "On?"

"The foundation. Your father's legacy. The pressure to get every decision right so no one questions you." Theresa's voice was matter-of-fact but not unkind. "It's a lot to shoulder."

Grace felt exposed, like Theresa could see through her rehearsed composure to the uncertainty underneath.

"I'm not shouldering it alone. I have the board. I have you. I have—"

"People who expect you to have the answers," Theresa finished gently. "When's the last time you were in a room where you didn't have to come up with solutions?"

The words hung in the air longer than Grace expected, settling somewhere she couldn't quite dismiss.

That evening, Grace sat across from Anna at their favorite neighborhood restaurant—a small Italian place where the owner knew their order and never rushed them through dinner.

Anna was telling her about a client case, something complex involving environmental law and corporate accountability. Grace tried to listen, but her mind kept drifting to the invitation sitting in her briefcase.

"You're somewhere else tonight," Anna observed, twirling linguine around her fork.

Grace blinked back to the present. "Sorry. Long day. Quarterly meeting."

"And the arts coalition request?"

Grace's fork paused halfway to her mouth. "How did you—"

"Because you've been carrying that check around like it's going to explode," Anna said with a gentle smile. "What's the holdup? It's exactly the kind of project you're passionate about."

Grace set down her fork. "My father used to say passion was a luxury we couldn't afford. That every dollar spent on what we wanted was a dollar taken from what someone needed."

Anna's expression softened. "And do you believe that? About this?"

Grace exhaled. "It's not about luxury or passion. It's about responsibility. I have a fiduciary duty—to the foundation, to the board. Shelters, food banks, job training—those are essentials. How do I justify putting half a million into art classes when people don't even have housing?"

Anna reached across the table, covering Grace's hand with hers.

"You know what your father also built? Beauty. The foundation's headquarters isn't utilitarian—it's gorgeous. The garden outside, the art in the lobby, the way he insisted on good coffee and fresh flowers for every board meeting? He knew beauty wasn't extra. It was its own kind of resilience – what makes life feel like living.... not just getting by."

Grace looked at Anna, her words rearranged something she'd been holding wrong.

"Your father didn't see the arts as frivolous," Anna continued. "He saw them as foundational."

Grace set down her fork, eyes flicking toward her. "That's not how he made it sound when I was growing up."

Anna brushed her fingers lightly against Grace's hand. "Maybe he wanted you to be practical. But I also think he believed beauty mattered. He just didn't have the words for it."

Grace looked away, throat tight. "Well, he gave me plenty of words about duty."

Anna held her gaze. "Duty, yes. But what if the word he really meant was stewardship? Not just weight on your shoulders—something entrusted to you, something you could shape."

The word clung to her long after dinner: *stewardship.*

Later that night, Grace sat alone in their home office, laptop open, staring at the foundation's financial dashboard. Numbers glowed on the screen—assets, allocations, impact metrics.

She opened a new browser tab and typed *"James Whitmore foundation articles"* into the search bar.

The results filled the screen: decades of profiles, interviews, and photos of her father at ribbon cuttings and award ceremonies, always smiling, always confident, always clear about his purpose.

She clicked on an article from over fifteen years ago, written just after her father's health scare – when she'd stepped in "temporarily" and never left.

"James Whitmore's approach to philanthropy is both methodical and deeply personal. 'Every dollar tells a story,' he explains. 'Our job is to make sure it's a story worth telling.'"

Grace scrolled down to a photo: her father standing in front of a mural painted by participants in a youth arts program the foundation had funded. His smile wasn't posed—it was genuine, proud, alive with possibility.

The caption read:

"Whitmore believes supporting the arts isn't separate from addressing poverty—it's integral to it. 'You can't sustain communities on survival alone,' he said. 'People need access to beauty and imagination, to remember they're more than their circumstances.'"

Grace stared at the photo, a sudden ache rising in her throat.

She wanted to call him, to ask him about that moment, about the decision to fund that program, about how he'd known it was right, even when the board probably called it a risk.

She wanted to hear his voice say her name with pride instead of constantly wondering what he would think.

But the silence stretched, and instinctively she filled it with the usual criticism—his, hers, it didn't matter anymore.

For the first time since taking over the foundation, she felt the full weight of what she'd inherited.

It wasn't just money or buildings or a board of directors. She'd inherited a philosophy, a worldview, a way of understanding what it meant to live a life that mattered.

But somewhere along the way, she'd started managing that legacy instead of living it.

She thought about the check still sitting on her desk, undelivered. The arts coalition wasn't misaligned—it was exactly what her father would have funded.

She'd called it prudence. Caution. But really, it was fear.

The ache in her chest wasn't grief anymore; it was longing. Longing to feel connected to the foundation's work again. Longing to make decisions from vision instead of doubt. Longing to honor her father by becoming who he'd raised her to be, not by preserving who he'd been.

She carried that restlessness into the night, and it was still there when she arrived at the office the next morning.

Waiting in her inbox was a subject line that stopped her cold: *"Because courage is contagious."*

She opened it, expecting another invitation or follow-up from a donor. Instead, it was from someone else entirely.

"Dear Grace,

My name is Dr. Sarah Kim, and I run the arts therapy program at the Children's Hospital. Last week, my eight-year-old patient Maya finished her cancer treatment and asked if she could paint a picture of what hope looks like. She painted a butterfly emerging from a cocoon.

Yesterday, I learned that your foundation is considering a grant to the Seattle Arts Coalition. I wanted you to know that what you're deciding isn't just about budgets or impact metrics. It's about kids like Maya, who need to create beauty even when—especially when—life feels impossible.

I'm attaching Maya's painting in case it helps you remember what you're really funding. Not art classes. Not nice-to-haves. Hope.

Gratefully,
Dr. Sarah"

Grace opened the attachment.

Maya's painting filled the screen—a burst of color and light. A butterfly with wings that looked like stained glass, emerging from what looked like darkness but wasn't frightening. It was anticipatory, like dawn breaking.

Grace stared at the painting for a long time.

Foundational, she thought, Anna's words echoing. *Not frivolous. Foundational.*

Then she picked up the phone and called the arts coalition directly.

"Hi, this is Grace Whitmore from the Whitmore Foundation. I'm calling about your grant request. I'd like to schedule a site visit. Today, if possible."

When she hung up, certainty settled in her chest.

Not the kind that came from having all the answers but the kind that came from trusting the questions.

That afternoon, Grace toured the Seattle Arts Coalition's after-school program in a converted community gym. The air smelled like rain and tempera paint. Coats dripped by the door, and someone had cracked a window to clear the fumes.

Kids moved between easels and folding tables, quiet but focused. A boy, maybe ten, in a paint-streaked hoodie was working on a small canvas, painting a fishing boat under a gray sky.

The instructor leaned in and told her his dad had been a fisherman—lost to a storm last year. The boy had found the photo on his mom's phone. "He says the sea behaves better in paint," she said with a small smile.

Grace stood there longer than she meant to, throat tightening. The boy's focus—the steady hand, the patience—reminded her of her father at his desk, pen moving across ledgers with the same deliberate care.

He wasn't painting for a grade or for praise. He was painting to make sense of something he couldn't fix.

The sound of rain filled the room, steady and patient. It had been a long time since she'd felt aligned with what she was doing.

When she left, she didn't second-guess it. She just knew.

When she returned to the office, Grace walked to Theresa's desk carrying the signed check.

"Seattle Arts Coalition," she said, setting it on Theresa's desk. "Please send this today."

Theresa looked up, eyebrows raised. "What changed?"

Grace thought about Maya's butterfly. About her father's genuine smile in that old photograph. Anna's words over dinner.

"I remembered that my father didn't build this foundation to preserve his legacy," Grace said. "He built it to amplify it. And sometimes, amplifying means taking risks on what might seem like extras but are actually essentials."

Theresa gave her a small, knowing smile. "Your father would be—"

"Making the same decision," Grace finished. "Just faster."

They both laughed.

As Grace walked back to her office, her heart felt full.

The simple recognition that she didn't have to choose between honoring her father's wisdom and trusting her own instincts.

She sat down at her desk and touched the celadon vase again, tracing those golden lines with her fingertips.

The cracks didn't make it fragile; they made it whole. Different from what it had been before, but somehow more beautiful for having been broken and mended.

Maybe that was what legacy really meant. Not preservation but transformation. Not keeping something exactly as it was but allowing it to become what it needed to be.

The phone on her desk was already ringing—probably someone with questions about the next board meeting or the dozens of other decisions waiting for her attention.

Grace picked up the phone more confidently, she wasn't bracing herself for the weight of other people's expectations.

She was ready to make important decisions that felt true, not just safe.

Because she knew that her decisions today would become the legacy she'd be proud to leave tomorrow.

And somehow, that felt like the most responsible thing she could do.

Ready or Not

the moment you realize every "yes" costs a version of you

SARAH'S PHONE BUZZED AT 5:43 A.M., JOLTING HER AWAKE. SHE fumbled for it in the dark, squinting at the screen. Unknown number. Probably spam.

She almost silenced it, then saw the name in the voicemail notification.

Rachel Winters.

Her body went very still.

Rachel Winters didn't make social calls. She didn't check in just to chat. If she was calling at 5:43 a.m., it was about work.

Sarah lingered over the voicemail icon, her pulse picking up at the thought of what waited there. She could delete it. Pretend she never saw it. Go back to the safe rhythm of school lunches and soccer schedules.

Instead, she pressed play.

"Sarah, it's Rachel Winters. I know this is out of the blue, but I have a situation I think you'd be perfect for. Meridian Health's new CHRO is looking for someone to lead a comprehensive retention analysis—specifically focusing on working parents. Six-month contract. Remote flexibility. And honestly? They need someone who understands what

these women are actually experiencing. I thought of you immediately."

A pause. Traffic sounds in the background.

"They're starting interviews next week, so if you're interested—or even just curious—call me back by Friday. I'd love to throw your name in the mix."

The message ended.

Sarah held the phone, her pulse hammering in her ears.

By Friday. Three days.

She set the phone down carefully, as if it might explode if she moved too fast.

For a moment, she just sat there in the dark, listening to Ethan's steady breathing beside her.

Rachel Winters. Her old boss. The woman who'd fought to get her promoted twice. The woman who'd said at her farewell lunch, *"When you're ready to come back—and you will be—call me first."*

That was seven years ago.

Sarah slipped out of bed, robe wrapped tight, and padded downstairs. The house was still, the kind of quiet that only existed in the hour before sunrise.

She made coffee—hands moving on autopilot—then stood at the kitchen sink, staring at nothing, or so she thought.

That's when she found Olivia's retainer in the garbage disposal. Not near it. Not beside it. In it. Wedged between the rubber flaps like some expensive piece of modern art no one ordered.

"How the hell?" she whispered to her kitchen ceiling, surgical tweezers in one hand and her phone flashlight aimed into the sink like she was performing emergency surgery. "I mean, how does a retainer end up in a garbage disposal?"

Call me back by Friday. Only three days.

The words pressed against her chest as she stared at the mangled pink plastic, still slick with dishwater.

For a long second, she just stood there, dripping hand suspended over the sink. The last week's version of her—the one who could turn any inconvenience into a full-blown lecture on responsibility—stirred, ready to snap to life.

But she didn't.

She rinsed it once under the faucet, set it on a folded paper towel, and looked at it—warped, useless, still vaguely disgusting.

Then, almost to herself, she said, "She'll figure it out."

The words surprised her. They didn't sound like defiance. They sounded like she meant them.

"What are you doing?"

Sarah jumped, nearly dropping the tweezers. Ethan stood in the doorway in his pajama pants and a faded college t-shirt, hair sticking up on one side.

"Finding Olivia's retainer," she said, gesturing to the paper towel. "In the garbage disposal."

Ethan blinked. Walked closer. Looked at the mangled pink plastic. Then looked at Sarah.

"How does that even—" He stopped, started laughing. The kind of genuine, bewildered laugh she hadn't heard from him in weeks. "I mean, how?"

Sarah felt her own laugh bubbling up despite everything. "That's what I said!"

"Did she, like, try to blend it?"

"I don't know!" Sarah shook her head, wiping her hands on a dish towel. "I genuinely have no idea."

Ethan leaned against the counter, still grinning. "Well, that's a two-hundred-dollar special."

"Don't." But Sarah was smiling now, too. "Don't make me laugh. I'm trying to be appropriately outraged."

"Are you, though?" He raised an eyebrow. "Because you seem weirdly calm about this."

Sarah looked down at the retainer. "Yeah, I don't know. Maybe I'm just too tired to spiral."

Ethan poured himself coffee, leaning back against the counter. "So what's the plan for today? I've got that conference call at nine, but I can move it if you need me to handle morning drop-off."

"No, I've got it. Olivia has early practice, Ben has a dentist appointment at eleven, but I already confirmed."

"Do you need me to take that?"

"I've got it."

"You sure? I can reschedule the call—"

"Ethan, I said I've got it." The words came out sharper than she meant.

He held up his hands. "Okay. Just checking."

Silence settled between them, not hostile but not comfortable either. Sarah wrapped both hands around her coffee mug, feeling the heat seep into her palms.

"I got a call this morning," she said quietly. "A voicemail. From Rachel Winters."

Ethan's eyebrows lifted. "Your old boss Rachel?"

"Yeah." Sarah took a sip, buying time. "She heard about a project. Six-month contract with Meridian Health. Retention analysis, focusing on working parents. Remote work, flexible schedule." She paused. "She wants to put my name in for it."

Ethan set his mug down slowly. "Wow. That's... wow."

"They're interviewing next week. She needs to know by Friday if I'm interested."

He nodded, processing. "Friday? Okay. So... what are you thinking?"

Sarah let out a breath she didn't know she'd been holding. "I don't know. I just got her call like an hour ago... It's been ten years, Ethan. Almost ten years since I worked. Since I was anything other than—" She gestured vaguely at the kitchen, the retainer, the chaos that was their life. "—this."

"You're not just 'this,'" Ethan said, but his voice was careful, like he was trying not to say the wrong thing.

"But what if I am? What if I interview and I can't do it anymore? What if I've forgotten how to be that person?"

Ethan ran a hand through his hair. "What about the kids? I mean, if it's remote, that's good, but six months is a commitment. How would we handle pickup? After-school stuff? What if one of them gets sick?"

There it was. The practical questions. The logistics.

Sarah felt something tighten in her chest, but she kept her voice steady. "We'd figure it out. That's what we always do."

"Yeah, but Sarah, I've got my own work. I can't just drop everything every time something comes up. You know my schedule—"

"I know." She cut him off gently. "I know your schedule, Ethan. I know exactly when you can and can't be available, because I've been managing around it for years."

She wasn't angry, just tired. "I'm not saying you don't work hard. I know you do. But you work, and I make it possible for you to work. That's how this has always worked."

Ethan was quiet for a moment. Then he set his mug down and looked at her directly.

"You're right. And I'm sorry if it's felt like I've taken that for granted." He exhaled. "Look, if you want to do this, I'm not going to stand in your way. We'll make it work. I'll adjust my schedule, we'll get more help, whatever we need to do. But Sarah?"

He waited until she met his eyes.

"This has to be your decision. I can't tell you what to do here. I can support you, but I can't want this for you. You have to want it."

Sarah felt the weight of his words settle over her.

It's your decision.

The phrase she'd been waiting for. The permission she thought she needed.

Except now, hearing it, she realized it wasn't permission at all.

It was responsibility. Handed back to her. Again.

"Okay," she said quietly. "I'll think about it."

Ethan nodded, kissed her forehead, and headed upstairs to get ready for work.

Sarah stood alone in the kitchen, coffee cooling in her hands.

She'd wanted his support. She had it.

But somehow, it still felt like she was carrying this decision alone.

She thought about the folder she'd found last week. The essay she'd written all those years ago: *"Reimagining Work as a Place of Belonging."*

She'd tucked them away, not ready to face what it meant. But now, standing in her dark kitchen with Rachel's voice still echoing in her head, she couldn't avoid it anymore.

Sarah opened the drawer and pulled out the folder.

The essay stared back at her, edges slightly worn, her own handwriting in the margins from years ago.

She carried it to the table, sat down, and began to read.

"What if we stopped treating work-life balance like a zero-sum game? What if belonging wasn't about fitting into

someone else's system but about building systems where people could thrive without disappearing?"

The words were hers. Clear. Confident. Unguarded.

She kept reading, pulled in by the voice on the page—a woman who believed her perspective mattered, who trusted herself to put ideas into the world without asking permission first.

"Retention isn't a benefits problem. It's a belonging problem. And until we create workplaces where people can show up fully—not just productively but humanly—we'll keep losing the talent we claim to value most."

Sarah beamed.

This was me.

She set the pages down and opened her laptop. The email from last week was still there—the one with the subject line *Reimagine What's Next*.

She opened the document she'd bookmarked but never completed.

The first question appeared, simple and piercing:

"Where in your life do you feel most like you've gone missing?"

Sarah stared at the blinking cursor.

Then she started typing.

"Everywhere. In conversations where I have nothing interesting to say. In photos where I'm either behind the camera or cut off. In my marriage, where I've become a logistics

coordinator instead of a partner. I've gone missing from anything that requires my opinion rather than my service."

The words came faster now, like something breaking open.

"What parts of your life no longer feel like yours?"

"My time. My voice. My sense that I matter beyond what I can do for other people. I used to have ideas. Opinions. Now I have thoughts about snack brands and carpool schedules."

"If nothing changes, what's the real cost to you—not just them?"

Sarah's hands paused over the keyboard. This was the question she'd been avoiding.

She typed slowly, each word heavy:

"I'll disappear completely. My kids will grow up thinking mothers are support systems, not whole people. I'll be fifty, then sixty, and I won't know who I am when I'm not needed. And the really scary part? I'll be so used to not mattering that I won't even miss myself anymore."

She stopped. Read it back. Everything clicked into place. It hurt.

She could see it more clearly now.

When I ignore my own needs, I drain every bit of energy I have. When I tell myself I'll wait until the kids are grown, I'm really just postponing my own life. And when I keep standing in the background, I teach everyone around me that my needs come last.

The essay lay where she'd left it. Rachel's voicemail blinked on her phone. Everything lined up, and the weight of it pressed down.

Friday. Deadline day.

That evening, after the kids were asleep and Ethan had retreated to his office, Sarah sat at the kitchen table, laptop open.

The essay glowed on the screen: *"Reimagining Work as a Place of Belonging."*

She'd read it a dozen times since finding it. Each time, the voice on the page felt more foreign and more familiar—like meeting a version of herself she'd forgotten existed.

She opened her email and started typing:

"Rachel—I got your voicemail. I'm interested. Can we talk Monday? —Sarah"

Her finger hovered over Send.

Sarah moved her cursor to Save Draft instead.

Not yet.

She closed the laptop and sat in the quiet kitchen, the weight of the unmade decision pressing against her chest.

The woman who wrote that essay was still here.

She just needed a little more time to remember how to speak.

The True Return

when success is measured by alignment, not approval

SARAH DIDN'T NOTICE THE SHIFT AT FIRST. BUT ONE SECOND, SHE was unloading the dishwasher, stacking mugs into the cabinet, and the next, her mind was somewhere else entirely. Not in her kitchen, not with the rhythmic clink of plates, but in fantasies of her standing in a conference room where a team was waiting for her to speak.

It was just a LinkedIn post—an old client celebrating the tenth anniversary of the system Sarah helped design. Ten years. She wondered if they still used her process, if anyone in that picture remembered the late nights, the moment she'd finally cracked the problem that transformed how the company viewed employee engagement.

The image sharpened inside her mind: her work bag draped over her shoulder, a crisp blazer, the heady rush of knowing she was the one with the answers. It was visceral, like she was right back in that moment, and it made her chest pulsate.

Then reality seeped in. *Maybe when the kids are older. If I find something part-time. We're finally in a routine—why stir the pot?*

The bargains stacked up as neatly as the dishes, but none of them settled the restlessness buzzing under her skin. She didn't want to give up the quiet mornings, the flexibility, the freedom to say yes to a last-minute lunch. But she missed the spark of creating solutions, the mental snap into focus when solving issues that mattered beyond the four walls of her home.

It wasn't that one role was better. They were just...different houses. And she was standing in the doorway, unsure which one to walk through.

She spent the rest of the day researching—not frantically but with a focus she'd forgotten she possessed. Career transitions. Women who'd rebuilt professional identities after years away. She wrote everything down, documenting evidence that reinvention was possible.

Time slipped away unnoticed. For the first time in years, she'd been so absorbed in something that wasn't about anyone else that she'd forgotten to check the clock.

She glanced up. "Shit! Ben."

She was supposed to be at his preschool ten minutes ago.

By the time she pulled into the parking lot, Ben was waiting by the curb with his teacher, clutching his dinosaur lunchbox, humming to himself. He climbed into his booster seat, chattering about snack time and how Rex got to "visit circle time again."

Sarah exhaled—half laugh, half self-reproach. "You're lucky your teacher likes us."

Ben grinned. "She said Rex is a good listener."

Traffic thickened as she made her way across town for Olivia's pickup. When she finally pulled up to the school, Olivia stood at the curb, ponytail slightly off-center, backpack hanging from one strap—the unmistakable look of a kid who'd been waiting only to feel wronged.

"Mom, you're late!" she announced, climbing in and tossing her backpack onto the seat with theatrics.

"I know, I know," Sarah said. "Traffic was awful."

It wasn't. She'd just lost track of time—a novelty in itself.

"Sorry, Liv." She caught her daughter's reflection in the rearview mirror—Olivia staring out the window, chin tilted high, exhaling loudly to make sure Sarah heard it.

The car ride home was quiet in that particular way only a nine-year-old could make it—no tantrum, no tears, just the pointed silence of disappointment. Ben played with his dinosaur, unbothered. By the time they pulled into the driveway, the weight of everything she hadn't done yet had settled on her shoulders like an old, familiar coat.

Sarah hadn't talked to Alexa in two days. That alone felt off—not because Alexa was a friend but because their exchanges were part of the rhythm she used to hold herself together.

"Alexa, play Norah Jones radio," she said, dropping her keys into the catch-all bowl.

"Now playing Norah Jones radio," the speaker chirped.

The slow, steady rhythm filled the kitchen. Safe. Familiar. She leaned against the counter, letting the first notes wash over her.

But the questions rushed back in.

What if I've let too much time pass? What if no one takes me seriously? What if the last decade was proof I've fallen behind?

The piano line drifted on—soft, steady, almost too composed. Nothing about this felt calm.

That's when she decided to run the numbers. She opened her laptop at the kitchen island, pulled up a blank spreadsheet and started typing: part-time nanny, transport, meal prep service, emergency coverage for sick days.

The total wasn't terrifying. It was doable.

But then the harder question came: Was buying back her time worth what she might miss doing it all herself?

The thought of missing the details—Ben's face lighting up when he spotted her in the pickup line, the quick five-minute chats with Olivia on the drive to dance class.

No one was trying to keep her home. But the gravitational pull of her family's needs and her finely tuned ability to respond made any attempt to step outside feel... expensive.

The word "expensive" echoed in her head all evening.

That night, after the kids were in bed, she called Kendra.

"You're alive," Kendra answered. "Last I heard, you were planning or thinking about coaching... no consulting? Did you do the thing without telling me?"

Sarah laughed. "No. Just... still wondering if I should go back to work."

"Okay, hold on. Before I jump in—do you want me to just listen, give advice, or hold up a mirror?"

Sarah hesitated. "Mirror, I guess. Even if I might not like what I see."

"Got it." Kendra's tone softened. "So... what's behind this? Excitement, fear, guilt—what's really driving this decision?"

Sarah twisted the phone cord between her fingers. "I miss parts of working outside the home—the challenge, the independence. But I also like the life I have now. I just... feel like I'm losing pieces of myself."

Kendra went quiet, letting Sarah's words hang there. Then she asked, "If we cleared away all the expectations—your kids, Ethan, the other moms—what would you choose for you? Not the version that makes sense on paper. The version that makes your stomach flip because it feels just like you."

Sarah let out a nervous laugh. "Honestly? I don't even know if I remember what I'd choose. It's been so long since the choice was really mine."

"So, what do you want? The real answer."

Sarah froze. No one had asked her that in years. Tears blurred her vision.

"I want something that's mine. And I'm terrified that makes me a bad mom."

There was a long pause on the other end. When Kendra spoke, her voice was softer now. "You're not a bad mom, Sar. You're just finally being honest. Maybe that's where you start—with the part you just said out loud."

Sarah couldn't find words. When the call ended, she pressed the phone to her chest as if that might muffle the question still ringing in her ears.

By the next day, the words still clung to her. *I want something that's mine. And I'm terrified that makes me a bad mom.*

She opened her laptop. The spreadsheet was still there. Her fingers moved almost without permission, typing two new headers: *For Me. For Them.*

The lists spilled out fast, unfiltered.

For Me: challenge, independence, adult conversation, money, a reason to put on real clothes before noon.

For Them: stability, consistency, availability, the comfort of knowing I'll be there—keeper of the family rhythm, emotional safety net, the one who makes life feel seamless.

She stared at the columns and saw what she'd been avoiding: This wasn't a budget problem. It was an identity problem.

If she stepped into a new role, what part of the old one would she be selling? Would the woman who always knew the details—the homework deadlines, the dentist appointments, which kid liked the crusts cut off—still exist if her time and attention were split?

The truth was evident: She wasn't just deciding whether to take on consulting clients. She was deciding whether she could still be the reliable center of her family and also be herself again—not just mom, not just steady, but whole.

She studied the columns until the words blurred. A spreadsheet wasn't going to solve this. What she needed was proof—proof that women like her, with gaps and kids and guilt, could still find their way back in.

That's when she scrolled to a name she usually avoided unless it was about the PTA: Marissa.

She remembered what Olivia had said at drop-off: something about "working from home isn't real work." Maybe Olivia hadn't understood it. Maybe Madison hadn't even meant it.

Still, it stung.

But maybe that was the icebreaker. It was safer than blurting out the question she actually wanted to ask: *What did you have to give up? Was it worth it?*

She typed, deleted, retyped.

"Hi Marissa—random question for you. First, Olivia brought home something she said Madison told her, and I wanted to clear it up. Second... I'm thinking about dipping my toe back into consulting and would love to hear how you make it all work. Any chance you'd grab coffee?"

She hit send before she could stop herself. The message whooshed away. Three dots appeared. Vanished. Reappeared.

Then: *"Yes to both. Tomorrow? 10 a.m. at Finch & Fig?"*

Sarah glanced back at the spreadsheet, pulse quickening. Asking for help shouldn't have felt this hard—but it did. It meant admitting she couldn't think her way out of this one.

The next morning, Sarah pushed through the door of Finch & Fig, her stomach twisting.

The café smelled like cinnamon and coffee. She scanned the tables, pulse quick, hoping Marissa would already be there so she didn't have to sit with her nerves.

Marissa was already there, two mugs on the table, hair swept into that efficient knot Sarah had secretly attempted for years.

"Hey," Marissa said, half-rising before she sat back down. For a moment, neither of them knew what came next.

Marissa lifted a hand. "Before anything else, I think I know what the comment was that Madison made to Olivia—can I explain?"

Sarah froze. "Uhhh, yeah... sure."

Marissa grimaced. "Madison overheard me after a nightmare Zoom call. A guy actually said, 'Well, you know, working in the home isn't real work.' I hung up and muttered, 'Right, apparently staying at home isn't real work.' Madison caught the sarcasm, lost the context, and... here we are. Was that it?"

Sarah let out a breath. "Oh, my god, yes! I was like, 'Why would Marissa say that?'"

Her cheeks burned. She'd built a whole story in her head.

"God, no. My whole M.O. is making sure women get humane

schedules and decent healthcare." Marissa slid one mug across the table. "Oat milk latte. Your text felt like an oat milk kind of text."

They both laughed—real laughter, the kind that loosened Sarah's shoulders.

Sarah took a sip. "Okay. Here's the thing." Her voice wavered. "I think I want to consult—HR strategy, retention, culture. But I'm... rusty. And it's not just that." She tapped the side of her cup. "It's the question that keeps circling: am I even relevant anymore?"

She let out a thin laugh. "And then there's the setup part— LLC, website, billing, that first 'Hi, I exist' email. I keep coming up with ideas, then find myself stopping. Half steps. Always half steps."

Marissa nodded. "I can only imagine. Honestly, that's the main reason I never stepped out...completely. I was worried about getting back in. But let me assure you—it's not as big a deal as it feels right now. Any workplace that gets you will be lucky to have you."

Sarah smiled sheepishly. "Thanks. It feels great to hear that from you. I've made some baby steps—I put a domain name in my cart, LinkedIn headline, draft only."

"Great baby steps!" Marissa said. "One foot in front of the other."

She flipped Sarah's napkin over and drew two columns. "Okay, let's run some scenarios. Money math and meaning math."

Meaning math? Sarah frowned. *What did that even mean— measured in guilt or hours of sleep?*

"Money math is tangible costs," Marissa said, writing. "Extra help with the kids. Systems to run the business. Cleaning services so you're not doing a second shift until midnight."

Sarah added excitedly, "Like maybe a photographer for head-shots if I want to look like a person who slept."

"Necessary!" Marissa wrote it down.

"Tangible returns," she continued. "Billable hours. Pipeline you control. The ability to say yes or no. Savings for Sarah's bucket."

"My own money?" Sarah said softly. "Ethan and I do all our finances together."

"That's not what I mean. I imagine there are times you feel 'guilty' for wanting to buy something for yourself? That feeling that you have to justify purchases through domestic duties. Catch what I'm saying?"

Sarah nodded slowly.

Marissa flipped the napkin. "Now, meaning math or intangible costs." She looked at Sarah. "Say them."

Sarah swallowed. "Less time after school. Fewer pickup hugs. Less influence over the house rhythm. The family losing the version of me that's always available."

"And intangible returns?"

Sarah watched the latte art blur. "Feeling fully awake again. Having adult conversations that show I know my stuff. Modeling for the kids—especially for Olivia—that women get to want things. Not outsourcing my ambition until ten years from now."

They sat with it.

Marissa exhaled first. "Okay, here's my unpopular opinion: the stuff in the second column-the feelings, the meaning- that should count more than the spreadsheet. The money part's straightforward. But the other part? That's what actually compounds. When you choose what feeds you, things start to open up. When you don't, the price shows up everywhere."

Sarah let the words settle in.

"Full disclosure," Marissa said. "Everyone thinks I have my act together. I don't. I have a support plan. My mom does two pickups. We have a sitter three afternoons a week. I missed Madison's last beam routine, cried in my car, then led a 6 p.m. client call with mascara on my wrist. I also love my work and what it allows me to do for our family. Both are true. I'm not less of a mom. I'm a mom who made a trade, and I keep checking if the trade still makes sense."

The honesty was refreshing. Finally, someone willing to drop the act.

"I've envied you," Sarah blurted.

Marissa didn't flinch. "I've envied you, too. The way you're actually *there*. The daily after-school hangouts, the unhurried stuff."

They laughed, and tension loosened between them.

Sarah pulled up an unsent email. "Would you... read this? It's to a former colleague who moved into consulting. I keep fussing with the subject line."

Marissa scooted closer. "'Subject: Exploring consulting— would love your take?' Clean. No apology." She scanned the body. "This is strong. You sound like you. You're asking for a fifteen-minute call, not a kidney."

Sarah breathed out. "What if she thinks I'm rusty?"

Marissa shrugged. "Then she'll be wrong, and you'll book with the next person. Hit send, then text me so I can send you three more names."

A small, private current ran through her.

Marissa clinked her mug against Sarah's. "There. Now it's real."

Sarah smiled. "It's... beginning."

On the walk to their cars, Sarah turned. "Thank you... for everything."

Marissa shook her head. "Don't mention it. It's what women do for each other. And if we don't, it's usually because we've been taught to see each other as competition when really, there's more than enough room for all of us."

Sarah leaned in for a hug, and Marissa's tight squeeze back stitched up something that had quietly come undone.

Back home, Sarah wrote the four napkin headers into her journal—*Tangible Costs, Tangible Returns, Intangible Costs, Intangible Returns*—and left space beneath each one.

Money math and meaning math. A way to count money and self at the same time.

The math on paper said yes. The math in her heart stayed divided, but the split no longer felt as raw. It felt like a seam— one she could mend, stich by stich as she figured out her way forward.

The questions she'd been avoiding were finally out in the open. She couldn't keep pretending the life she had was the same as the one she wanted.

Over the next week, she opened her journal daily to review her intangible costs and returns. She took time to feel what was missing, to trust her own intuition.

This wasn't about numbers. It wasn't even about logistics.

It was about asking herself a question she'd been avoiding:

Which version of me do I want to grow into?

She didn't have the answer. And maybe she didn't need it yet.

The decisions didn't have to come all at once. The relief came in realizing she could stand at this crossroads without sprinting toward one path just to quiet the discomfort.

There was electricity in that space. Not tidy, not certain, but alive.

Tomorrow would look the same on the surface—school drop-off, groceries, emails. But she knew *she* had shifted.

She was starting to see her life with distance now—starting to notice where she'd been standing too close. And once you see the shape of the crossroads, you can't unsee it.

The house was quiet in that particular way that it only got after 9 p.m.—kids asleep, Ethan in bed working. It was the hour when her thoughts finally lined up, when courage felt possible.

She sat in the living room, Cooper's head warm against her feet, laptop open, the printed essay beside her.

"Reimagining Work as a Place of Belonging."

Her cursor blinked at the end of the title. She began typing, line by line, transferring what she'd once written—pausing now and then to add, revise, soften. The woman who'd written it years ago had ideas. The one typing tonight had perspective.

Just publish it.

Her voice echoed: *"Don't wait for the perfect moment. Just put it out there."*

Sarah opened LinkedIn. The blank post box stared back.

Her fingers moved before she could stop them:

"I wrote this years ago, before I convinced myself my perspective didn't matter. I was wrong. Here's what I've learned about building workplaces where people—especially moms—can belong."

She attached the essay below.

Then stopped.

The old voices rushed in:

What if no one reads it? What if they think you're naive? What if people judge you? What if Ethan thinks you should have asked him first?

Her hand moved to close the tab.

But then she thought about Olivia.

About that morning weeks ago, when her daughter had asked, *"Why don't you go to work like Madison's mom?"*

About the look on Olivia's face when she'd said, *"My mom doesn't give speeches."*

Sarah's nails dug into her palm.

She thought about what she'd written in her journal that morning, pulled from the email prompt:

"If you stay invisible in your relationships, what do you teach the people who love you?"

What am I teaching Olivia about what women get to want?

Her daughter was watching. Learning. Absorbing the unspoken lessons about whose voice mattered—and whether her own would be one she could trust.

Sarah looked at the screen again—at the introduction, at the Post button.

She thought about the woman who'd originally written those words. Curious. Opinionated. Unguarded.

That woman's still here. She's just been waiting.

She didn't count to three. She didn't make a list. She didn't text Kendra or Marissa for one last reassurance.

She just clicked.

For a split second, the button turned gray, processing. Then—

"Your post is live." The words appeared on the screen like a fact she couldn't take back.

Sarah's heart slammed against her ribs.

For a second, nothing happened.

What did I just do?

Her body hadn't caught up yet—hands buzzing, breath shallow, that shaky mix of fear and relief that always followed doing the hard thing.

Her phone lit up with a text alert about five minutes later.

Marissa: *"I KNEW you had this in you. Call me tomorrow."*

Sarah let out a breath.

Another notification fifteen minutes later. A comment from someone she didn't recognize:

"This is exactly what I needed to read today. Thank you."

Then another.

"Sharing this with my entire HR team."

Sarah stared at the screen, tears blurring the words.

It wasn't viral. But it was real.

People were reading it. Responding. Not to the polished version of herself, but to the truth.

She set the phone down and closed the laptop.

She'd done it.

Not perfectly. Not without fear.

But she'd done it.

Sarah padded down the hall, stopping outside Olivia's room.

She pushed the door wider and stepped inside.

Olivia was sprawled across her bed, one arm flung over her stuffed giraffe, breathing soft and steady.

Sarah sat on the edge of the bed.

For a long moment, she just watched her daughter sleep—this fierce, opinionated, beautiful girl who was learning every day what it meant to be a woman in the world.

Sarah brushed a strand of hair from Olivia's forehead.

"You get to want things," she whispered. "Big things. Scary things. Things that don't make sense to anyone but you."

She paused, voice catching.

"I'm still learning that, too."

Olivia stirred but didn't wake.

Sarah pulled the blanket up over her daughter's shoulders and walked quietly to the door.

I did this for you. But I also did it for me.

Back in her bedroom, Sarah climbed into bed, the weight of the day finally settling into her bones.

Ethan was already asleep beside her.

She picked up her phone one last time.

Three more comments. Two shares. A message from a former colleague: *"Sarah Greene! Are you consulting now? Let's talk."*

She locked the screen and set the phone on the nightstand, face down.

Tomorrow would be another ordinary day. But there would also be emails to answer. Conversations to have. A future to build that included all of who she was—not just the parts that served everyone else.

Sarah closed her eyes, exhausted but awake in a way she hadn't felt in years.

She didn't know what came next.

But she wasn't waiting for permission to find out.

She'd begun again.

The Toll of the Mask

*when financial success becomes
emotional bankruptcy*

THE HOUSE HAD FORGOTTEN HOW TO BE STILL. MATEO WAS HOME
again, and with him came all the things Elena told herself she
missed—wet towels on the bathroom floor, the fridge left hanging open, half-empty water glasses everywhere.

She thought it would feel grounding, comforting, like proof
that she hadn't lost her place in his orbit.

Instead, it made her restless.

The phone at the dinner table, doors closing hard enough to
make a point, the word "good" standing in for a whole conversation. Three seconds of eye contact, then he was gone again, back
upstairs, back to whatever world didn't include her anymore.

Elena sat in her home office, laptop open, eyes darting
between the glow of her inbox and the timer on her phone.
Nearly 7:30 p.m.

She'd promised herself she would stop working at seven.
Dinner together, just the two of them, no distractions. She'd even
taken chicken out that morning, marinated it, and lined up the
vegetables like some aspirational food blogger.

And yet her fingers found the trackpad anyway, pulling up
one more email like a reflex she couldn't name.

The red dots blinked in the corner of her screen. She stared at them, wondering what would happen if she just stopped answering.

"Mom?" Mateo's voice floated down from upstairs. "Coach said you still need to sign the tournament form."

She winced. "It's on the desk in your room," she called back. "Don't forget to pack your cleats."

A pause, then, "Obviously."

He sounded older now, more efficient, as if he didn't need her reminders anymore. But she still gave them, like conditioned responses she couldn't unlearn.

She wanted to climb the stairs, peek into his room, linger until he gave her a real answer about his day.

But the moment she pictured it—him looking up, half-smile fading into a sigh heavy with irritation—she froze.

If she stopped too long, she might actually feel it- the hollow space where their connection used to be, and how much of him had grown up while she was looking the other way.

She turned back to her laptop, telling herself she'd spend time with him after finishing this last update.

Only, one update turned into six.

By the time she shut the screen, the chicken she'd marinated that morning sat forgotten on the counter, and Mateo's room was dark — another night that had come and gone.

The competing desires were constant, like two voices fighting for space inside her ribcage.

I want to step back—for Mateo, for myself, for the chance of something more than this treadmill I'm on.

If I step back, everything I've built will slip away. Clients will notice. Staff will lose confidence. And maybe that's the real fear – that it won't.

Lately, Mateo had started to notice, too. The tension she thought she was hiding had begun to leak through the seams.

"You're not even listening," he'd snapped over dinner a few nights earlier, pushing his plate away.

Her fork clattered. "Of course I am."

He gave her that look—half disbelief, half exhaustion—that was becoming more familiar every day.

Then he disappeared upstairs, leaving her staring at the abandoned plate.

She knew he was right. She wasn't really listening. Not to him. Not to herself.

The bargaining loops played on repeat, like a machine she couldn't unplug.

Once this development deal closes, I'll slow down.

It's just a busy season. I'll recalibrate later.

If I take a real break, people will wonder what's wrong. If I admit I'm tired, they'll think I'm slipping.

So she kept going—one more email, one more proposal— telling herself balance was coming. Just not today. Never today. Tomorrow she'd be different. Tomorrow she'd stop choosing work over everything else.

Every cell in her body ached for rest. But her brain wouldn't stop scrolling through the mental tabs she'd left open: contracts, closings, Mateo's slipping grades, the half-finished conversation with Seth.

Her phone buzzed just as she was shutting down her laptop. Seth's name lit up the screen.

For a moment, she considered letting it go to voicemail—she didn't have energy for the kind of honesty he always pulled out of her.

She answered anyway.

"I knew you'd be awake," his voice was low and easy, a reminder there was life beyond the deals and the distance.

"Hi," she said, aiming for casual, though it came out softer than she intended.

"Look, I know you've got a crazy week," he began, "but what if we did something low-stakes? A dinner tomorrow. No strings. Just... see where things go."

Elena's instinct was to reach for the same script: *Busy week. Deadlines. Next time.*

But something caught her in the pause – the slow, unexpected breath that filled her all the way up.

"Yes, let's do that."

Maybe she just wanted to be somewhere she didn't have to manage the mood, read the room, or shape-shift into whoever was needed next.

By the time she pulled into the narrow parking lot, she'd stopped pretending it was harmless.

The restaurant was small and dimly lit, with exposed brick walls and jazz playing low in the background. It was nothing like the upscale hotel lounges she was used to.

Seth was already there, leaning back in his chair like he belonged, two tumblers of bourbon sweating on the table.

"You actually came," he teased when she walked in.

She rolled her eyes, sliding into the seat opposite him. "Don't sound so surprised."

The banter came easily, surprisingly so. Within minutes, she was laughing—real laughter, not the polite kind she offered in client meetings.

He asked questions that didn't belong in the usual small talk. What did she cook when she was only cooking for herself? Who was the last person who made her laugh so hard she cried? If she could disappear for a weekend, where would she go?

She found herself answering honestly, surprised by the ache it exposed—how long it had been since someone wanted to know her, not what she could do for them.

For four hours, she let herself relax. She even silenced her phone, sliding it face-down on the table—a small gesture but so foreign it felt like rebellion.

And she enjoyed herself, *really* enjoyed herself.

The warmth in her chest wasn't just from the bourbon; it was from being seen.

The crash came later.

By the time she got home, the night had settled, but her to-do list hadn't. The bar's warmth still clung to her skin as the familiar glow of her laptop replaced it.

Her inbox had tripled—two client calls "just checking in," her assistant forwarding a contract flagged for errors, a reminder for Mateo's parent-teacher meeting she'd already rescheduled twice.

Just a quick scan. Just to make sure nothing was on fire.

But the second the laptop opened, her body remembered its favorite shape. Shoulders tensed. Breath held. Her brain clicking into the version of herself that knew exactly what to do.

One email became three, then ten. Each response a small dose of dopamine —proof she was essential, irreplaceable, still the one the business depended on. The warmth from earlier evaporated. This feeling was sharper, more familiar.

This was the part no one warned her about—the whiplash of wanting something different but being too entangled in who she'd become to let go.

Desire had a cost. Hers was paid in hours she'd never get back.

She sat there staring at the screen, willing her hand to close the laptop.

Just close it. Walk away.

But she didn't. She couldn't.

When she finally crawled into bed, it was nearly three.

Morning came hard and heavy. Mateo was already halfway out the door when she stumbled into the kitchen, eyes gritty, body aching from too little sleep and too many demands.

"You okay?" he asked, a note of curiosity under his teenage nonchalance.

"Yes, fine," she said too quickly, reaching for her phone before she even poured coffee. "Just a late night."

He hesitated at the door. "You always say you're fine. You don't look fine."

By the time he left, the weight had returned. The illusion of ease she'd felt the night before vanished, leaving only the ache of everything waiting for her.

Even her team noticed. When she bit someone's head off over a typo in a deck—a typo—the associate went very still. That look. The one she recognized from childhood, when her mother's moods turned after too many double shifts. It was the look that said people had to tiptoe around her.

Later, Seth checked in. *"Last night was fun. Let's do it again soon?"*

She stared at the message, the reply button blinking like a dare.

For a second, she almost typed *"yes"*—but the familiar pressure crept back in.

One night off and it already felt like everything might come undone.

She locked the screen instead.

That evening, while Mateo clattered dishes in the sink, Elena stood at the counter holding a contract she couldn't focus on.

She was somewhere else. Replaying the last twenty-four hours.

The lightness she'd felt sitting across from Seth who wanted to know her. How quickly that ease had curdled into panic – the inbox explosion, the snapping at her team, the impossible math of being present for Mateo while also being who her clients needed.

One breath. That's all she'd taken. One night of letting go.

And the cost had been immediate.

The truth she'd been outrunning finally caught up: the security she'd built – the business, the reputation, the identity as someone who never dropped a ball – wasn't freedom at all.

It was a trap disguised as success. And she was both the prisoner and the warden.

All that proving hadn't kept her safe. It had just kept her pinned in place, saying yes to everything except her own life.

When that realization hit, she did what she always did.

She reached for the wine.

Not for pleasure. For pattern. For the thing that came next in the sequence of her evenings. A ritual she'd dressed up as self-care.

The soft click of the glass meeting the counter. The weight of the bottle in her hand. The first sip slid warm down her throat – it was a forced relaxation.

But as the wine spread through her chest, the thought she'd

been holding at arm's length all day slipped through:

What if this is it? What if you've built a life you can't afford to step away from? What if letting go means watching it all fall apart?

And underneath that, even quieter:

Or maybe you never will.

Elena returned home – to the business. She leaned back in her chair, eyes fixed on the rows of numbers blinking back at her: profit margins, commissions, projections she'd triple-checked.

They told the story everyone else wanted to believe: growth, stability, influence.

She should have felt calm. Instead, her stomach tightened— the quiet ache of knowing that order wasn't the same as peace.

Her phone buzzed—another congratulatory message from a colleague. *"You're unstoppable, E. I don't know how you do it."*

The words should have felt like praise. Instead, they landed like a dare: *Don't stop now.*

Because Elena knew scarcity when she saw it. She'd grown up inside it. Her mother in the checkout line, pretending to read the magazine rack while silently watching the register tally. Her father's voice tight with panic, snapping about lights left on, doors left open.

Back then, scarcity was loud—visible, humiliating.

Now it was quieter, more cunning.

It didn't live in her bank account anymore; it lived under her skin.

It whispered that slowing down meant slipping back. That rest was just another word for becoming irrelevant.

She was rich. The house was paid off. Mateo's college fund secure. She could stop tomorrow, and financially, nothing would change.

But *rich* was never the point, was it?

What she craved wasn't money—it was validation. Proof she was still relevant. Still exceptional. Still the kind of woman people relied on.

Somewhere along the line, financial security stopped being about protection and started being about performance. And this is how women like her vanish—applauded all the way down. Celebrated for their tireless work. Admired for never stopping. Praised for the very addiction that's killing them softly.

Vanessa had tried to name it years ago. Over lattes, she'd looked Elena dead in the eye and said, "You're rich, E. But you're starving."

Elena had laughed—too sharp, too fast—and smoothed the cuff of her blazer like that was the thing out of place.

"I'm not starving," she'd said. "I'm ambitious."

But the word *starving* stuck like a burr.

Ambition was supposed to lead to freedom, wasn't it? To more space, not more spinning. To ownership, not obligation.

Yet the more she built, the more confined she felt, like every new property, every deal, every client tied another thread around her, until she couldn't tell if she owned the business or if it owned her.

The numbers on the screen were absurd. Once, she would've called them financial freedom.

But instead of relief, all she felt was the tightening.

Because that number wasn't freedom—it was a contract that said, *"Keep hustling. Keep going. Don't you dare stop."*

Vanessa was right. She was starving.

Just not for money.

Under it all was the fear she'd been running from: if she slowed down, if the calendar finally cleared, she'd be left sitting across from her son with nothing but time—and no idea how to bridge the distance she'd let grow between them.

What if she'd been so busy being essential to everyone else that she'd made herself optional to the one person who actually mattered?

She pressed her eyes shut, but silence was already speaking.

The next morning, Mateo padded into the kitchen, hair sticking up in every direction.

"Morning." He poured cereal into a bowl, barely looking at her as she sat on a wooden stool sipping her coffee.

Mateo grunted, his face in his phone. He smiled at something she'd never know about. A whole life was happening in there—jokes, friends, heartbreaks, maybe—and she was no longer the person he brought them to.

"You've got practice tonight?" she asked.

He nodded. "Yeah. Sierra's picking me up."

The flicker of jealousy was immediate and sharp. She covered it with a sip of coffee. "That's nice."

Mateo shrugged, spoon clinking against the bowl. "Hmmm, I guess."

She tried to keep the conversation going.

"Coach still making you run laps for being late?"

"Nah," he said, eyes still on his phone.

She nodded, searching for questions but came up empty.

Funny. She could charm a room full of investors, but couldn't make it through a breakfast without losing him to the scroll.

Later that day, Elena sat in her car outside a listing appointment, looking every inch the woman who had it all together.

Her phone lit up. Another client. Another request. Another confirmation that she mattered.

She should have felt victorious.

Instead, she felt tired in a way sleep couldn't fix.

You're rich, but you're starving.

Vanessa's words played on repeat, and Elena finally let herself hear them. Really hear them.

She was starving. And she knew exactly what would feed her—time with Mateo, space to breathe, permission to be ordinary, a life that didn't require her to work late nights and weekends.

But knowing what you need and having the courage to reach for it are two entirely different things.

So she grabbed her purse, checked her reflection one last time, and got out of the car.

The machine kept running. And she kept feeding it the only thing she had left: herself.

That night, Mateo sat across from her at the kitchen island, half-heartedly pushing pasta around his plate. He was quieter than usual, which wasn't saying much. But the distance tonight felt heavier.

"You've been at Dad's a lot lately after school," she said, trying to keep her tone light.

He shrugged. "Yeah. It's just... easier."

The words hit like a sucker punch. She tried to swallow the pain down, tried to keep her expression neutral. "Easier how?"

"I don't know." He twisted his fork, eyes still on the plate. "He's just... there."

And you're not.

The words he didn't say hung between them, louder than anything he could have spoken.

Elena forced a smile, like she could rewrite the moment into something salvageable. "Well, I'm here now."

He nodded, but the look on his face said everything. He didn't believe her. And why should he?

Later, when she heard Mateo's shower turn on, she poured herself a glass of wine and opened her laptop.

Emails stacked in her inbox like bricks in a wall she couldn't stop building.

It was always the same bargain: *I'll put in a few extra hours tonight so I can be free tomorrow.*

Tomorrow never came.

Friday night, while negotiating a contract, she received a message from Seth.

"Still up? Thought about grabbing a nightcap."

The word *"yes,"* was right there, easy. She could use the company. The distraction. The possibility of something that wasn't work or worry or wine alone at home.

Instead, she watched the screen until it went dark.

Because saying yes meant more than a drink. It meant letting someone close enough to see the cracks. To ask the questions she didn't have answers for. To let him see the part of her that didn't have it all figured out.

And she wasn't ready for that.

Maybe she never would be.

Her mother called. Elena answered, bracing herself.

"*Mija*, how are you? How's Mateo?"

Elena leaned against the kitchen table, closing her eyes. "He's fine, *Mamá*. Busy with soccer."

"And you? Are you fine?"

The question was too simple, too direct. Elena let out a soft laugh. "I'm working, like always."

"*Ay*, Elena." Her mother's sigh carried years of this same conversation. "You work too much. The moments don't come back, *mija*. You know this"

Her throat tightened. "I know, *Mamá*."

"Do you?" A pause. "Your abuela used to say something—*'Rica en todo, pobre en vida.'* Rich in everything, poor in life. She said it about the families she cleaned for in Guatemala. Big houses, beautiful things, nice cars. But no one was ever home. No one laughing. Just empty rooms full of expensive things."

Elena's throat tightened.

"You're building those same houses now, mija. You sell them to people just like that. But you know what scares me?" Her mother's voice dropped. "You're living in one."

The silence stretched.

"You have everything we worked for you to have. Everything. But what do you have that matters? What do you have that you can't buy?"

Elena couldn't answer.

"That's what I'm afraid of," her mother said quietly. "That you'll have everything—and nothing at all."

After they hung up, Elena stood at the living room window with her glass of wine, watching the lights in her neighborhood blink like distant stars.

Somewhere out there, people were living slower lives. Maybe fuller ones.

She pictured Mateo at Derrick's house, laughing over dinner in a way he didn't anymore with her. She imagined Seth at some bar, ordering that nightcap—maybe with someone braver, someone who said yes.

She could have been a different woman. Could have chosen differently.

But here she was. With her wine and her house and the business she couldn't let down.

She told herself she'd change. After this quarter. After this deal. After Mateo's season wrapped.

Later.

Always later.

The word was a lullaby she'd been singing herself for years —a promise that let her keep going without ever actually changing.

As the weekend wore on, nothing outwardly changed. Elena closed deals, smiled in client showings, and missed Mateo's tournament game.

But the slow unraveling was there, quiet and steady.

In the way Mateo didn't tell her how the game ended.

In the way her stomach tightened when she turned out the light, the silence of her bedroom pressing down on her.

She wasn't falling apart.

She was holding it together so tightly that there was no room left to breathe.

On Sunday evening, Elena sat on the couch, laptop balanced on her knees, screen glowing in the dim room.

Mateo was upstairs. Door closed. Playing videos games when he should have been sleeping.

She thought about knocking, about telling him it was time for bed.

Her hand hovered over the laptop.

She could close it. Walk upstairs. Try.

Instead, she searched the MLS.

A few minutes later, she heard him laugh —a sharp, genuine sound she hadn't heard directed at her in months. She glanced at the ceiling. He was probably texting friends. Or his dad.

People who actually knew the young man he was becoming.

She heard his room go silent and she understood what it meant: he'd heard her down here. Knew she was home. And chosen a buffer of darkness over her company.

When had that shift happened? When had she become someone he managed rather than sought out?

She knew the answer. She just didn't want to look at it directly.

Her phone buzzed. A text from Derrick: *"Mateo asked if he could stay here next weekend again. That cool with you?"*

She started at the message.

That cool with you?

As if it mattered. As if Mateo had asked her first. As if she were still the parent he turned to.

She typed back: *"Of course. Whatever works for him."*

The response was immediate: Thanks. He's doing great, by the way.

He's doing great.

At his dad's house. Where things were easier. Where Sierra was always there.

She set the phone down, screen dark.

Upstairs, Mateo's dark room served as a wall between them that she'd helped him build. One missed dinner, one distracted conversation, one "just a minute, honey" at a time.

She closed the laptop.

The air in the room felt suffocating.

And she realized—he wasn't waiting for her anymore. He'd stopped hoping she'd show up. Stopped expecting her to choose him over the work.

He'd adapted. Moved on. Found what he needed elsewhere.

It was easier for him that way.

Less disappointing.

The thought sat in her chest like a stone.

She could go upstairs right now, she knew he was still awake. Knock on his door. Try to repair what she'd let fracture.

But what would she even say? What could possibly undo months—years—of him learning that her phone, her clients, her deals would always come first?

So she stayed on the couch.

Tomorrow, she told herself. I'll try tomorrow.

The word was a permission slip she'd been signing for years.

Upstairs, she heard Mateo walking around.

And in the space between them, nothing changed.

Worth Without Performance

when power comes from presence, not proving

By Monday morning, it wasn't the packet itself that unsettled Ava—it was how clean they'd made it look. Ten years of exemplary performance distilled into a manila folder labeled "restructure."

Not fired. Not free.

Repositioned. Like a chess piece someone else was done using.

She'd skimmed the first pages and understood: "Client Services Division" meant keep the work, lose the power. Build someone else's empire—the firm's reputation, the client relationships that made partners rich—but never own any of it.

The work. The grind. The dead ends.

Without the power, the visibility or the path forward she'd been promised.

At 7:02 a.m., she called Claire in. "You get one, too?"

There was a pause, then the sound of Claire's breath catching. "Yeah. Mine says 'Operations Support.'"

Ava pressed her fingers against the knot forming in her neck. "So, it wasn't just me."

"Nope." Claire's voice was flat, resigned. "Safe job. Small pay cut. You know the drill."

Safe.

Ava almost laughed. Safe was code for sidelined. For *we don't need you where it matters anymore.*

"Jenna got one too?" Claire continued. "Four years supporting David, stellar reviews. They moved her to Operations Support last month. Suddenly now, she's leaving."

Ava frowned. "Leaving the team?"

"Leaving the company. Maybe the workforce entirely." Claire paused. " She says its for her family. That's the headline, anyway."

Ava felt something cold settle in her stomach. "But?"

"But let's be real—if men were getting pushed out like this, nobody would call it a family decision. They'd call it what it is."

The word Claire didn't say hung between them: displacement.

Ava read the articles—record numbers of women leaving the workforce. They made it sound voluntary, like an awakening. Women choosing family over corner offices, opting out of the rat race.

But sitting here, packet on her desk, it didn't feel like choice.

It felt like being quietly shown the door and asked to say it was your idea.

She wrapped up with Claire and opened her laptop, staring at her inbox.

She could email Emily from HR right now: *"Thank you for the opportunity. I accept."*

Clean. Done. Over

Her fingers hovered over the keyboard.

Instead, she opened LinkedIn. Job postings scrolled past in a blue blur: *Senior Portfolio Manager. Director of Client Strategy. Vice President of Growth.* Same titles. Same salary bands. Same bullet points she could recite in her sleep.

She'd done all of it. Exceeded all of it.

And the thought of clicking "Apply" made her stomach twist.

What if it's just more of the same? Different office. Same game.

She closed the laptop and walked to the window.

Below, the city moved in its Monday morning patterns: taxis cutting through traffic, people clutching coffee cups like lifelines, everyone moving with purpose toward something.

For a moment, she envied them. How certain they all looked. How productive.

Then the thought arrived, unwelcome: *What if they're just like you? Too busy proving they can handle it to ask if they even want it.*

She pressed her forehead against the cool glass.

Ten years of this. Ten years of believing that if she just worked harder, delivered more, proved herself again and again, eventually it would pay off.

And here she was. Demoted in all but name. Replaceable.

The system hadn't failed her.

It had worked perfectly—used her exactly as designed, then discarded her the moment she'd served her purpose.

Her phone buzzed. A text from David: *"Don't forget Henderson follow-up today. CC me when you send draft."*

Ava let out a short, sharp laugh.

Of course. David still expected her to carry the work – even with the demotion packet on her desk, still warm from Friday's bloodbath.

She typed without thinking: *"Not my account anymore. Ask Bryan."*

She started at the message.

Too honest. Too risky.

She deleted the words and replaced them with two safer ones: *"Got it."*

She hit send. Her jaw ached from clenching.

She stared at the two words – *Got it* – the same two words she'd typed a thousand times before. A reflex. A survival mechanism. A way of swallowing everything else she wanted to say.

Got it meant: I'll do the work you should've assigned to someone else.

Got it meant: I won't make this awkward for you

Got it meant: I know my place.

And just like that, the pattern continued.

Different day. Same compliance.

She set the phone down, hands shaking slightly.

By noon, she'd run the mental loop a dozen times.

Take the role, play it smart, let the dust settle.

But later turns into forever. You know that.

Be grateful. You still have a job.

At least. The language of women who settle.

What if you say yes and disappear piece by piece, until there's nothing left but the version that plays nice?

She was wrung out from arguing with herself. Jaw sore. Right foot tapping a relentless rhythm under the desk. Her whole body buzzed with adrenaline that had nowhere to go.

Finally, she dragged the folder closer and forced herself to read the letter again:

"*We are thrilled to invite you to continue your journey with Bridgewell Partners in this exciting new role.*"

She snorted. "*Thrilled. Exciting.*"

The title stared back at her: *Director, Client Services Division.*

Technically lateral, but everyone in the business knew it wasn't.

Client Services was where they put people they were done with but couldn't afford to fire. A glass box. She'd see the deals, hear the strategy, watch younger people – mostly men – do the work she used to own.

But never touch it again.

She imagined introducing herself at the next industry event: *"I'm in Client Services now."*

The polite nods. The brief pause. The mental asterisk people would add: *Oh, she used to be someone.*

Her stomach turned. This wasn't a role. It was a slow professional death dressed up in benefits and PTO.

Late that night, Ava laid on her back, staring at the ceiling. LinkedIn on her phone, casting shadows across her face in the dark.

She scrolled through the same job postings again. Not applying. Not deciding.

Suspended.

Her stomach twisted every time she imagined saying yes to the packet. But saying no terrified her more.

Take the job. At least you'll look stable.

Stable is just another word for stuck.

You don't walk away from steady income. Not in this economy.

You don't build the life by clinging to scraps.

Her heart pounded. It was like arguing a case where both sides were right.

She set the phone face-down and pressed her palms over her eyes.

"I don't know what I want."

If felt terrifying to admit. But also—for the first time in a long time—honest.

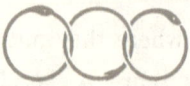

By 6:30 a.m., she was at her desk. Coffee steaming, inbox at zero. She still woke at 4:15 without an alarm, still prepped client decks no one asked her to touch. Still triple-checked every comma like her career depended on it.

Because for years, it had.

The habits had carved grooves so deep that even now—demoted, sidelined, stripped of power—she couldn't stop.

She forwarded résumés for colleagues who hadn't asked. Emailed Claire an over-thought response to a client question Claire could've handled herself. Spent two hours refining a pitch deck for a meeting she wasn't invited to.

Her hands moved. Her brain solved problems. Her body exuded productivity.

But none of it mattered anymore.

And she couldn't stop doing it anyway.

By 8:00 a.m., the office started filling in. The usual wave of navy suits, voices buzzing, laptops snapping open.

Normally, this energy fed her—proof that the machine was running and she had a place in it.

But this morning, the sounds made her skin prickle.

The machine was still running.

Without her.

She passed David in the hallway. He smiled, easy, like nothing had changed. "Morning, Ava."

Her voice came out too bright, too eager. "Morning! Big day ahead?"

As if enthusiasm could disguise the fact that she had no part in it.

David nodded absently, already turning toward another EVP,

already deep in conversation about something that no longer included her.

She stood there a little too long, like proximity alone might pull her back into relevance.

Then she turned back to her office. The walk felt longer than it should have.

By noon, she realized she hadn't eaten. She'd spent the whole morning manufacturing work—updating her LinkedIn profile, refreshing her inbox, creating a project plan for a team she no longer led.

Each keystroke a plea: *See me. Need me. Keep me.*

Her colleagues drifted past in clusters, headed to lunch. No one asked if she wanted to join.

They probably assumed she was too busy. That was the reputation she'd built: Ava, the fixer, the one with no time for anything but work.

The irony burned—she was drowning in time and starving for connection.

By midafternoon, she couldn't sit still anymore. She walked the floor hunting for problems to solve. A client deliverable waiting for review? She inserted herself. A junior analyst's messy slide deck? She offered edits no one asked for.

Phantom echoes of who she used to be.

She lingered outside a conference room where a strategy meeting was underway. Her old team sat around the table, heads together, markers flying across the whiteboard.

Someone glanced up. Saw her through the glass.

She smiled-polite, professional—and kept walking.

But her chest felt hollow.

She couldn't stand being on the other side of the glass. Watching the work happen without her. Irrelevant in the place where she used to matter most.

By 5 p.m., the office thinned out. People gathered their keys and jackets, already planning dinner, happy hour, the gym.

Ava stayed at her desk, eyes locked on her screen.

She started drafting the handoff notes. Client summaries, status updates, next steps. The polite choreography of being replaced.

She told herself it was professionalism—making sure nothing slipped through the cracks. But each email was its own quiet surrender, one more relationship she'd built and was now signing away.

At 7:00 p.m., she finally packed up. The security guard nodded as she passed through the lobby. Outside, the city was alive with people heading somewhere that mattered.

She stood on the curb, work bag cutting her shoulder, and realized she had nowhere to go.

Home was just another empty space. And the office—the place she'd given everything to—didn't want her anymore.

So she stood there.

Between two places that didn't feel like hers.

That night, Ava ran the numbers again.

The math was supposed to be simple. Numbers didn't lie. Numbers kept you safe.

But tonight, the numbers felt like quicksand.

Same base pay, smaller bonus, no equity. Less access. Less status. Less everything.

She'd run the calculations four times already. Her fingers moved through the cells— recalculating, re-checking, as if the formula might suddenly deliver a different answer.

It didn't.

If she stayed, at least she could count on the stability. Predictable deposits. The condo, the dinners, the "oh, Ava's doing so well" at family gatherings.

If she left, that column stayed blank. No formulas. No projections. Just a void her brain couldn't compute.

Her stomach tightened.

She remembered her first promotion, years ago. The way her father had told the neighbors, chest puffed. *"My daughter, the youngest VP in the division."* The pride in his voice had been intoxicating.

The fear now wasn't just about money.

It was about what those numbers meant: safety, legitimacy, proof she had arrived.

She typed a new scenario: *What if she downsized? Sold the condo, moved somewhere smaller?*

She deleted it—fast, like closing an embarrassing browser tab. *Downsizing felt like failing.*

She scrolled to her savings account. Calculated how long she could last without a paycheck.

The numbers should have felt more than sufficient. Six months. Maybe eight if she was careful.

But the ledger in her head said deficit – no matter how high the balance climbed.

She tried to picture life without the corporate card, the priority boarding, the quiet relief of knowing she could afford anything she wanted.

The images wouldn't form. Her mind refused to see them.

For one dangerous moment, she let herself imagine it: walking away. Saying no. Not having to prove or perform or calculate every choice against a spreadsheet.

The thought felt like stepping off a cliff.

She snapped the laptop shut.

But the panic didn't stop when the screen went dark. If anything, it grew louder.

She curled onto her side, pulling the duvet to her chin, heart racing.

If the numbers can't keep you safe, what can?

The question followed her into restless sleep.

Wednesday morning, Ava opted to work from home. She sat at her kitchen table, coffee going cold, disoriented on all the options for her future in her laptop.

The HR email in her inbox, unanswered.

Her phone buzzed. A text from Sophia: *"Coffee today? I'm in your neighborhood."*

Ava's first instinct was to decline. She had nothing to report, no clear decision with options to present.

But recycling all the same information repeatedly felt futile. At least Sophia would have perspective.

She typed back: *"11 a.m?"*

They met at a corner café, the kind with mismatched chairs and chalkboard menus. Sophia was already there, laptop closed, hands wrapped around a mug.

She smiled when Ava walked in. "You look exhausted."

Ava slid into the chair across from her. "That obvious?"

"Only to someone who's been there." Sophia pushed a latte across the table. "I ordered for you. Whole milk, extra shot."

Ava's throat tightened at the small kindness. "Thanks."

They sat in silence for a moment. Then Sophia leaned forward.

"So. What's going on?"

Ava hesitated. Then the words came tumbling out—the packet, the demotion disguised as lateral movement, the calculations she'd been running for days, the paralysis.

Sophia listened without interrupting.

When Ava finally stopped, Sophia asked quietly, "What do you want to do?"

"I don't know." Ava's voice cracked. "That's the problem. I've spent my entire career knowing exactly what to do next. And now? Nothing feels right."

"What feels wrong about taking it?"

Ava stared into her coffee. "It makes me feel small. Like I'm agreeing that I'm worth less now. That all those years of work didn't matter."

"And what feels wrong about walking away?"

"Everything." The word came out sharper than she intended. "The gap on my resume. The questions. The instability. What if I can't find anything else? What if this was my peak and I didn't even know it?"

Sophia nodded slowly. "Can I ask you something?"

"Yeah."

"What would you tell someone else in this situation? If a friend came to you with this exact problem, what would you say?"

Ava opened her mouth. Closed it.

The answer should have been easy. But sitting here, trying to imagine giving advice she couldn't take herself, the words wouldn't come.

"I don't know," she finally admitted.

"That's because you're still trying to solve it like a work problem," Sophia said gently. "Like there's a right answer if you just run the numbers enough times."

Ava felt something crack open in her chest.

"But this isn't a spreadsheet, Ava. This is your life. And the question isn't 'what's the smart move.' It's 'what kind of person do you want to be?'"

Sophia was quiet for a moment, then leaned back in her chair. "You want to know what I wish someone had told me when I left?"

Ava nodded.

"That the hardest part isn't making the decision—it's knowing how to make it. You're running the numbers, weighing the risks, building the case. And all of that matters. But when those things don't give you a clear answer, when the spreadsheet comes out even, that's when you realize you're missing something." She paused. "This isn't just a career decision – it's a values decision. You need both sides of the equation to choose something you can actually live with."

Ava felt something loosen in her chest.

"When they reassigned me," Sophia continued, "I already knew I was done. I'd been unhappy for a while, so I started working with a coach and mapping out options. I was about to pull the plug anyway. So when they offered the demotion, I told them to give it to someone else. Then I gave myself six months—not to find the perfect job, but to figure out what I actually wanted. I joined a women's network for people in transition, said yes to every coffee meeting that sparked my curiosity. Not just the ones that looked good on paper."

"And what happened?"

"I took some time off before stepping into my new role," Sophia said. "Not to check out—but to finally slow down to hear myself think. I focused on resetting my nervous system first— sleep, movement, breath, the basics I'd ignored for years. Once I wasn't running on fumes, I could finally see the pattern: I'd built a career around proving, not choosing. From that clearer place, the plan came easily. I knew what kind of work I wanted, what kind of leader I wanted to be, and what I wasn't willing to tolerate again."

She smiled slightly. "Turns out, when you stop running, the next step gets a lot clearer."

Ava swallowed hard. "Did you ever regret it?"

"Leaving?" Sophia considered. "No. But I regretted not doing it sooner. I regretted all the years I knew it wasn't aligned—yet kept trying to earn respect from people who were never going to give it to me."

She paused, thoughtful. "Honestly, the only real regret I have is not trusting myself sooner. I used to think I was a master decision-maker—I made calls that moved millions, solved other people's problems for a living. But when it came to my own life, I realized I didn't have a framework. I didn't know how to make decisions for *me*—the kind I could actually live with."

She pulled out her phone and started typing. "I'm sending you something. A few questions from the woman I worked with when I was figuring out my next move—they stopped me in my tracks. She also connected me with a community that changed everything. It's women who are in that in-between space—where you know something has to shift, but you're not sure what comes next. It's real. No posturing."

Ava's phone buzzed with the messages.

"And one more thing," Sophia said, her voice gentler now. "You're going to want to make this decision from fear—fear of the gap, fear of what people will think, fear of not being enough without the role. But here's the thing: the fear doesn't go away when you stay stuck. It just gets quieter. And that's the kind you should really watch out for."

"Why?"

"Because when fear gets quiet, you mistake it for peace. You start telling yourself you've accepted reality—when really, you've just stopped fighting for what you actually want."

Ava felt tears prick her eyes. "I don't even know what I want anymore."

"That's okay. You don't have to know yet." Sophia reached across the table and squeezed her hand. "But you do have to stop letting other people decide what you're worth. Whether you stay or go, change careers of just take a breath—that part has to end."

They sat in silence for a moment, the café buzzing around them.

Then Sophia added, almost as an afterthought, "Oh—and block your calendar. Seriously. Protect your time, even if you don't know what you're saving it for yet. That was the hardest part for me —realizing my time still had value, even when I wasn't producing or getting paid for it."

Ava thought about her calendar—every slot marked "available," every weekend on call, every evening "just in case."

Sophia watched her for a moment. "It's not about overhauling your life overnight," she said. "Just start small. One afternoon that's yours. One choice that's for you, not for anyone else. See what happens."

Ava walked home slowly, Sophia's words circling in her mind. She'd spent years trying to think her way forward. Maybe this time, she'd try something different – maybe it was time to feel her way back to herself.

Her phone buzzed.

A text from her sister: *Emma's dance recital is Friday. I know you're probably working or busy, but she asked if you'd come. No pressure.*

Ava stared at the message.

No pressure.

Her sister always said that. And Ava always had an excuse ready—client meeting, deadline, emergency. All valid. All true. All bullshit.

Her fingers moved: *I'll try to make it.*

She stopped.

I'll try.

The language of hedging. Of caring just to the point of appearing thoughtful—but never to the point of letting anyone down.

She deleted it.

For a long moment, she stared at the blinking cursor.

Then typed something different:

I'll be there. Front row. Tell Emma I wouldn't miss it.

Her heart pounded as she hit send.

No hedge. No escape hatch. Just a promise.

The response came immediately: *Really? Ava, she's going to be so excited!! Love you and can't wait to finally see you, it's been way too long!*

It was such a small thing. A dance recital. Two hours on a Friday.

But it felt enormous.

Because for once, she'd said yes to something that didn't earn her a title or a gold star.

She'd said yes to just showing up.

She opened her calendar and blocked off Friday afternoon: *Emma's recital.*

Then, before she could second-guess it, she kept going.

Saturday morning: *Offline.*

Sunday: *Offline.*

Her stomach clenched. *What if someone needs you? What if there's an emergency?*

But underneath the panic, quieter: *What if there isn't?*

Outside, the city moved with its usual urgency. Inside, she let herself sit in the quiet.

She hadn't answered HR. Or applied for new jobs. But something had changed.

She'd drawn a line – not around her career, but around her life.

And this time, she meant to follow it.

The Third Path

*when wealth becomes who
you are, not what you have*

THE DEPOSIT CONFIRMATION EMAIL ARRIVED.

"Check deposited on behalf of the Seattle Arts Coalition
—$500,000."

A green check mark blinked back at Grace from the screen,
cheerful and final.

She held her mug to her lips without drinking, steam rising
between her and the monitor.

For a moment, relief loosened the knot under her sternum. *Done.* The thing she'd been circling for months was now a
line item in the ledger.

Then the second feeling slipped in, quiet as a draft:

Was that the right move... or just the one I wanted to be right?

She had the authority to approve it. But authority didn't mean
immunity. The board could question her. Richard could still call
it out of line.

She swiveled her chair toward the bookshelf so her back faced
the door.

Inside the office, the faint floral note of the fresh arrangement Theresa insisted on each week. On the sill, the celadon vase
caught the morning light, gold veins gleaming along its repaired
fractures.

Her father had believed in preservation—protecting what was already built, maintaining the legacy, never risking it.

But Grace was learning that real stewardship wasn't about keeping things intact.

It was about making space for what came next.

The Seattle Arts Coalition wouldn't fix everything. Not the reputation she'd inherited, not the compromises she'd made to get here.

Grace turned back to the screen and reread the confirmation, as if a second pass might reveal an escape clause she'd missed.

The money was gone. The decision was made.

Her cursor drifted to her calendar.

Board finance call next Tuesday. Development committee Wednesday. Donor stewardship on Thursday.

Saturday: *Whole Woman Wealth.*

The invitation had been sitting in her desk drawer, tucked beneath a stack of grant proposals. She'd almost deleted the calendar reminder three times.

An intimate virtual reflection circle for women who've built extraordinary lives and want to be sure their values still match the lives they've created.

Grace stared at the blue square on her screen.

She didn't do circles. Didn't share her doubts with strangers who'd inevitably compare notes later, measure her choices against their own, wonder if she'd earned the seat she occupied or just inherited it.

She certainly didn't need a facilitator with a meditation bell asking how she *felt* about legacy and leadership.

But her fingers hovered over the delete button without clicking.

Maybe it was Theresa's words: *"When's the last time you were in a room where you didn't have to have the answers?"*

Maybe it was exhaustion.

Maybe it was the fact that she'd been second-guessing herself for eighteen months – ever since her father got sick and she became the only voice in the room that mattered.

Before, there had been someone to test ideas against. Someone who knew the history, understood the stakes, could tell her when she was being too cautious or too reckless.

Now there was just her. And the weight of every decision with no one to share it with.

She moved her cursor away from delete. Left the blue square exactly where it was.

On her desk sat two binders, each labeled in Theresa's precise handwriting:

Plan A – Strategic Continuity

Plan B – Bold Expansion

She'd been working on them for months. Opening them, closing them, running the numbers again. Telling herself she was being thorough when really, she was stalling.

Plan A was preservation: incremental growth, proven programs, her father's vision sustained. The board would approve it unanimously. His legacy would remain intact.

Plan B was transformation: cultural equity initiatives, arts funding, programs that couldn't be measured in neat quarterly reports. Riskier. Messier.

Hers.

Both plans were defensible. Both had the data to back them up.

But only one required her to believe she had the right to remake what her father built.

She reached for a sticky note and wrote: *Review both options after next board cycle. Stewardship requires patience.*

She pressed it onto the folder and closed it.

The familiar exhale—the relief of postponement.

She told herself it was wisdom. Due diligence. Respect for what came before.

But sitting in the quiet of her office, she knew what it actually was.

Fear that choosing Plan B meant trusting her own judgment over his. And after a lifetime of following his lead, she wasn't sure she remembered how to trust herself.

Saturday morning arrived gray and heavy, Seattle wrapped in its familiar mist.

Grace made coffee, changed clothes twice, and sat down at her desk ten minutes early, laptop open, camera off.

The Zoom room was thoughtfully designed—a soft neutral background, gentle instrumental music playing as women joined, names appearing one by one in elegant font. Intentional without being fussy, warm without being performative.

Eight women total.

Grace kept her camera off, cursor hovering over the leave button.

At exactly 10:00 a.m., a woman appeared on screen—steady voice, presence calm but certain.

"Good morning," she said. "I'm glad you're here. I know showing up to something like this takes courage."

Grace shifted in her seat, skeptical.

"Before we begin," the woman continued, "let me say what this circle is—and what it isn't.

This isn't therapy. It's not a workshop where I give you five steps to fix your life. It's simply a space to pause, to name what's true, and to remember you're not alone in what you carry.

"The point isn't to fix anything," she added. "It's to notice what's true before you decide what comes next."

She paused, letting the words settle.

"We're going to go slow. No one has to share anything they're not ready to share. You can keep your camera off if you need to. But I will ask you to stay present—not multitasking, not checking email. Just here."

Grace's hand moved away from the leave button.

"Let's start with something simple," the woman said. "Turn your camera on if you're comfortable and share your first name and one word for how you're feeling right now. Just one word. No explanation needed."

One by one, faces appeared on screen.

"Rachel. Tired."

"Amara. Uncertain."

"Sophia. Skeptical."

Grace hesitated, then turned her camera on.

"Grace. Cautious."

The woman smiled gently. "Thank you for your honesty."

The first hour moved slowly, deliberately. The questions felt deceptively simple.

"What brought you here today?"

"What season are you in right now—creation, refinement, expansion, or recovery?"

The women spoke carefully at first, testing the water.

A CEO talked about inheriting her family's company and feeling like an imposter.

An artist talked about financial success making her feel disconnected from her work.

A lawyer talked about achieving everything she'd set out to achieve and still feeling empty.

Grace listened.

These women didn't know each other. They were strangers on a screen. And yet there was something in their voices—the same exhaustion, the same longing—that felt uncomfortably familiar.

Then the facilitator asked the question that changed everything.

"I want to ask you something that might feel uncomfortable," she said, her tone soft but direct. "And you don't have to answer out loud if you're not ready. But I invite you to sit with it."

She paused.

"What are you protecting by staying where you are?"

The silence stretched.

One by one, the women began to speak.

"I'm protecting my father's reputation," the CEO said quietly. "If I change things, people might think he did it wrong. And I can't... I can't let that happen."

Grace's throat tightened.

"I'm protecting the idea that I have it all figured out," the lawyer said. "If I admit I don't know what I'm doing, people will stop trusting me."

"I'm protecting myself from being visible," the artist whispered. "If I stay small, no one can criticize me."

The facilitator nodded slowly. "When you think about what you've been protecting," she asked, "what part of you benefits from it?"

No one spoke at first. But the question lingered.

Then her gaze softened toward the screen—not singling anyone out but inviting everyone in.

"Grace," she said gently. "What about you?"

Grace's pulse thudded in her ears.

She almost said nothing. Almost turned off her camera. Almost left the call.

But something in the CEO's words—*If I change things, people might think he did it wrong*—had cracked something open.

"I'm protecting myself from being wrong," Grace said, her voice barely above a whisper.

The facilitator nodded. "And what would it cost you to be wrong?"

Grace blinked, her vision blurring.

"I'd disappoint people. The board. Donors." She stopped, her throat closing. "My father."

"Your father," the facilitator repeated softly. "Is he here?"

Grace shook her head. "No. He passed."

Kate nodded, her voice softening. "When we lose someone—especially someone whose approval shaped so much of our life—it can take years before our decisions feel fully our own again. Grief blurs confidence. You start second-guessing yourself, hearing their voice in your head every time you move forward."

She paused, letting the truth breathe.

"And sometimes, without meaning to, we keep asking for their permission. Not because we're weak—because we haven't learned how to trust our own voice in the silence they left."

Grace's breath hitched.

"What if the voice in your head—the one that questions every move, the one that tells you you're not ready or that you'll disappoint him—what if that isn't his voice at all?" the facilitator said quietly. "What if it's fear trying to keep you safe, trying to protect you from another loss?"

Grace's breath caught.

She'd never thought of it that way.

The rest of the circle passed in a blur—more stories, more truths, more women naming what they'd been carrying alone.

But Grace couldn't stop thinking about Kate's question.

What if it's fear trying to keep you safe?

When the circle ended, Grace sat in the quiet of her office, staring at the black screen.

Her hands were still shaking.

She stood and walked to the window, legs unsteady.

Outside, the mist had lifted. Joggers moved along the waterfront in steady rhythm.

Grace pressed her palm against the glass, feeling the coolness seep into her skin.

Something had shifted.

Not fixed. Not resolved. But shifted.

For the first time in months, she didn't feel alone in the weight she was carrying.

She thought of the CEO, voice cracking as she talked about protecting her father's reputation. The artist, terrified of being visible. The lawyer who had everything and still felt empty.

She thought of herself—standing outside boardrooms, writing postponement notes on sticky pads, circling the same decision because she was terrified of choosing wrong.

What are you protecting by staying where you are?

Grace closed her eyes.

She was protecting herself from the possibility that she wasn't ready. That without her father's approval—real or imagined—she had no right to lead, to change anything, to trust her own judgement.

But what if Kate was right?

What if the voice she'd been listening to wasn't his at all?

Grace turned to the celadon vase. She'd kept it in the office, thinking it would help her feel connected to him.

But maybe she'd been looking at it wrong.

The vase wasn't beautiful because of the gold threads. It was beautiful because someone had honored the breaking – and chosen to make something new from it.

She picked up her phone and texted Eun-Ji. *"Can I come by?"* The response came immediately. *"I'll put the kettle on."*

Grace arrived at her aunt's Madison Park townhouse just as the sun was setting, the sky streaked with pink and gold.

Eun-Ji opened the door before Grace could knock, as if she'd been waiting.

"Come in, Grace-ah."

Inside, the air smelled faintly of ginger and incense. The walls were lined with books, not color-coded or arranged for show just stacked and lived-on. A kettle whistled softly from the kitchen.

Eun-Ji motioned toward the low table where two celadon teacups sat waiting, pale green with hairline cracks running through the glaze.

"Sit," she said simply. "Tea first. Talk after."

Grace sank onto the floor cushion. The tension in her body loosened.

Eun-Ji poured the tea slowly, deliberately, the steam curling upward. She handed Grace a cup, the ceramic warm against her palms.

Neither spoke. The only sound was the clink of glass.

Finally, Eun-Ji spoke.

"Do you know what wabi-sabi is?"

Grace nodded. "Beauty in imperfection."

Eun-Ji smiled, small but amused. "Close. But it's more than

that. Wabi-sabi means accepting change. It means seeing the chipped bowl, the fading flower, the cracked cup—and letting them be. Not trying to fix them. Not hiding them. Just... letting them exist as they are."

She gestured to the teacup in Grace's hands.

"These cups are old. Worn. Imperfect. But they're more beautiful because of it, don't you think?"

Grace traced the hairline cracks with her fingertip, the gold glaze catching the light.

"Your father struggled with that," Eun-Ji continued. "He wanted everything to run smoothly. To reflect well on the family. He thought that's what success looked like – control, perfection, nothing out of place."

Grace looked up. "But he kept that celadon vase in his office. The kintsugi one."

Eun-Ji nodded. "Yes. My friend Kenji gave it to him. Kenji taught us about wabi-sabi, about kintsugi – the art of repair. He wanted your father to understand that strength isn't about never breaking. It's about what you do after."

Grace had to clear her throat before speaking. "I never knew that."

"Your father didn't talk about it much," Eun-Ji said softly. "But he kept that vase on his desk every day. I think, in his own way, he was trying to learn the lesson."

Grace set down her teacup, reflecting on her morning.

"I approved the Seattle Arts Coalition grant. Half a million. And I went to a women's circle today," she said quietly. "I almost cancelled but didn't."

Eun-Ji's eyes flickered with interest. "And?"

"Someone asked me what I'm protecting by staying where I am." Grace's voice cracked. "And I realized... I'm still asking for his permission. Even though he's gone. I keep imagining what he'd think, what he'd say, whether he'd approve. And I've been so afraid of disappointing him that I've... stopped trusting myself."

Eun-Ji reached across the table and took Grace's hand.

"Grace-ah," she said gently. "You think you're honoring your father by preserving everything exactly as he left it. But that's not what he wanted."

Grace looked up, tears blurring her vision.

"How do you know?"

Eun-Ji stood and disappeared into the other room.

When she returned, she was holding a small silk pouch, faded and delicate with age.

She sat down across from Grace and placed the pouch on the table between them.

"Your father gave this to me three weeks before he died," Eun-Ji said softly. "He asked me to wait until you were ready. He said I'd know when that was."

Grace stared at the pouch, her pulse quickening.

"What is it?"

"Open it."

Grace's hands trembled as she loosened the silk ties and reached inside.

Her fingers closed around something small and cool. She pulled it out slowly.

A pendant. Delicate, traditional, unmistakably Korean. The metalwork was intricate—a small lotus blossom, edges worn smooth with age and use.

"It was your grandmother's," Eun-Ji said quietly. "She wore it when she left Busan. When she came to this country with nothing but two children and a suitcase. She gave it to him before she died."

Grace's vision blurred. "I had no idea this even existed."

Eun-Ji nodded. "He kept it all these years. He wanted you to have it."

Grace held the pendant up to the light, watching it catch the glow from the lamp. The lotus petals were worn, the chain delicate but strong.

"There's something else," Eun-Ji said gently.

She opened an envelope pulled out a folded piece of paper, yellowed at the edges, creased from being opened and refolded many times.

Grace took it with shaking hands and unfolded it carefully.

Her father's handwriting. The familiar loops and slants she'd grown up seeing on birthday cards and notes left on the kitchen counter.

Grace-ah,

If you're reading this, it means Eun-Ji believes you're ready. I trust her judgment—she's always seen you more clearly than I could.

By now, you've probably spent months (years?) trying to figure out what I would have wanted. You've probably questioned every decision, afraid of dishonoring what I built.

Let me save you the trouble: I don't want you to preserve what I built. I want you give it new life.

The foundation isn't the legacy, Grace. You are.

My mother wore this pendant when she left everything she knew to build a life she couldn't yet imagine. She was terrified. She didn't speak the language. She had no money, no connections, no safety net. But she went anyway because staying meant limited opportunity for her children.

I kept this pendant for you to remind you of that courage.

The courage to become something new, even when it means leaving the old behind.

I changed my name because I thought I had to. Maybe I was right. Maybe I was wrong. I'll never know. But what I do know is this: I didn't build the foundation so you could spend your life protecting it. I built it to live on in you—not as a burden, but as a beginning.

Legacy isn't keeping everything exactly as I left it. It's you— carrying forward what matters and letting go of what doesn't.

Wear this pendant. Carry us with you—me, your grand- mother, all the people who loved you into being. But don't carry our rules. Carry our values. And then make them your own.

You were always ready, Grace. You just needed to believe it.

사랑해, 아빠

(I love you, Dad)

Grace's hands shook so hard she had to set the letter down.

The tears came fast and quiet, spilling over before she could stop them.

She pressed her palms to her face, shoulders shaking.

Eun-Ji moved around the table and sat beside her, wrapping an arm around her shoulders.

"He knew," Grace whispered through her tears. "He knew I'd be afraid."

"Of course he knew," Eun-Ji said softly. "He was afraid too— when he changed his name, when he started the foundation, when he handed it to you. Fear doesn't mean you're doing it wrong, Grace. It means you're doing something that matters."

Grace picked up the pendant, holding it against her chest.

The foundation isn't the legacy, Grace. You are.

She thought of her grandmother leaving Korea with nothing but courage and a suitcase. Her father becoming James Whitmore, building something from nothing. Herself, standing at the edge of a choice she'd been too afraid to make.

"I've been asking the wrong question," Grace said quietly. "I keep asking what he would have wanted. But maybe the real question is: what do I want to create?"

Eun-Ji smiled, squeezing her shoulder. "There she is."

Grace wiped her eyes, a quiet laugh escaping through the tears.

"You belong to a lineage of women who reinvented themselves," Eun-Ji said. "Your grandmother. Your mother. Me. And now you. That's what you're doing too."

Grace nodded, clutching the pendant.

They sat together in the quiet, teacups cooling, incense smoke curling upward.

Finally, Grace stood, slipping the pendant over her head. The lotus rested against her collarbone, cool and grounding.

"Thank you, Auntie."

Eun-Ji smiled. "Go build something beautiful, Grace-ah. He's already proud of you."

Grace drove home slowly, the pendant warm against her skin.

She didn't go straight to bed. Instead, she sat at her kitchen table with the letter in front of her, reading it once more.

You were always ready, Grace. You just needed to believe it.

She traced the edge of the paper, her father's handwriting blurring slightly in the low light.

Then she stood, walked to her desk, and picked up the two binders.

Plan A. Plan B.

She held them for a moment, feeling their weight.

Then she set Plan A aside and opened Plan B.

By Monday morning, something had shifted.

Grace woke early, the sky still gray with dawn. She made coffee, showered, dressed carefully.

Then she sat down at her desk.

The two binders were still there: Plan A and Plan B.

She opened them, scanned the pages one final time.

Then closed them both and set them aside.

She opened a new document and typed at the top:

Plan C: A Vision for Our Next Chapter

Her fingers moved steadily, the words flowing without hesitation.

Plan C honors what's worth carrying forward: my father's belief that beauty, meaning, and service are not separate from survival but essential to it.

Plan C also creates what's mine: the courage to fund what can't always be measured, to trust instinct alongside data, to allow transformation instead of demanding preservation.

This isn't about protecting what was. It's about stewarding what could be.

She listed the initiatives: expanded arts funding, cultural equity grants, storytelling programs, creative entrepreneurship support, community-driven design.

She included the data. The metrics. The projections.

But she also included the stories. Maya's butterfly. The boy in the hoodie. The laughing in the arts studio.

Because courage is contagious.

When she finished, she saved the document and printed it.

Then she slipped the pendant out from beneath her blouse, holding it in her palm.

Her grandmother's. Her father's. Now hers.

She tucked it back beneath her collar, the lotus resting against her heart.

By 9:45 a.m., Grace stood outside the boardroom, Plan C tucked under her arm.

Through the glass walls, she could see them gathering: Richard adjusting his cufflinks, Helen reviewing notes on her tablet, Sanjay tapping his pen against the table, Michelle pouring coffee with a quiet smile.

Grace's pulse thudded in her ears.

Her hand moved instinctively to the pendant at her collarbone, feeling the small raised edges of the lotus through the fabric of her blouse.

She thought of Kate's question: *What's worth carrying forward, and what's yours to create?*

She thought of Eun-Ji pressing the pendant into her palm. *You belong to a lineage of women who transformed themselves. Now it's your turn.*

She thought of her father's letter. *The foundation isn't the legacy, Grace. You are.*

Inside, the board was waiting.

Richard would have questions. Sanjay would push back. Helen would want reassurances. Michelle would support her.

But for the first time, Grace wasn't presenting someone else's vision.

She touched the pendant one more time—cool, grounding, hers.

Then she opened the door.

And walked in.

Epilogue

I WROTE THIS BOOK BECAUSE I KNEW I WASN'T THE ONLY ONE holding these questions in the quiet. Questions about the kind of success we're told to chase, the kind of power we're taught to shrink ourselves for, and the kind of wealth we're expected to measure in numbers when what we're really aching for is meaning.

I spent twenty years inside the wealth management system—a system designed without women's voices, choices, or lives in mind. I've lived the invisible rulebook about success, power, and wealth. And I've worn every version of it.

As the divorced woman starting over, I rebuilt my life from a one-bedroom apartment and less than one hundred dollars in my checking account.

As the stepmother to three boys, I tried to balance ambition with presence, traveling up to three weeks a month for an executive position, while missing moments I knew I'd never get back.

As the high achiever, I chased the next rung like oxygen, blind to the fact that there was no finish line—only a moving goalpost that kept me running while my joy lagged further behind.

And as the legacy builder, I wrestled with the question that kept me up at night: How do I make wealth mean more—not just for my family, but for every woman trying to live with intention?

Here's the truth no one tells you: The cost of living by someone else's definition of success isn't just burnout or lost time. It's the quiet erosion of your own voice. It's waking up to a life that looks impressive on paper but feels unrecognizable to the woman you thought you'd be.

You've met four women in these pages, each facing a different version of the same crossroads.

One stayed in the cage she built, even after she saw the door was open. She chose control over connection, performance over presence. She had everything she worked for—and lost everything that mattered.

One drew her first boundary after years of erasing herself in service. She's still figuring out who she is when she's not needed—but she's finally asking.

One stopped trying to earn her worth through endless proving. She hasn't mapped her future, but she's reclaimed her time. And that's where transformation begins.

One walked into the boardroom carrying both her father's legacy and her own vision. She stopped asking for permission she didn't need and started trusting the authority she'd always had.

Four different choices. Four different outcomes.

But the question underneath was the same: *What does it cost to keep living by rules that were never written for you?*

Maybe you recognized yourself in one of them. Maybe you saw pieces of all four.

Either way, you're here now. Eyes open. Heart awake.

And once you see the pattern clearly, you can't go back to not knowing.

This is where the shift happens. Not in grand declarations or perfectly mapped plans, but in the everyday moments that reveal who we're all becoming.

It's the day a woman walks out of a meeting, leaving a promotion on the table because the cost to her health and marriage is too high.

It's sitting across from a divorce attorney, realizing the settlement she's about to sign is the first time she's ever truly chosen herself.

It's saying no to the client who drains her energy, even though the paycheck is tempting.

It's taking a Wednesday afternoon off to pick her kids up from school—not as a guilty indulgence, but as a deliberate choice.

Women with a clarity that makes compromise impossible, a confidence no longer tethered to acceptance, and a conviction that outlasts the pull of old rules.

This is the work. Not a one-time declaration. Not a box you check. But a return, again and again, to your own truth.

We are living in a time when the systems that promised women safety, belonging, and recognition—marriage, the corporate ladder, the "perfect" home—are showing their cracks.

If you've ever looked around at a life that was supposed to make you happy and thought, *This can't be it*, you know what I mean.

If you've ever felt the quiet panic of realizing you've followed all the rules and still feel unseen, you've lived it.

If you've ever thought, *I've built everything I was told to want... so why does it feel like I'm disappearing inside it?*— you've already met the truth I'm talking about.

The rules we inherited for success, power, and wealth were not written with us in mind.

But here's what I know now, after two decades of living inside those rules and another decade of helping women rewrite them:

The old blueprints are crumbling. And what rises next depends on the choices we make—not someday, but now.

This isn't just about your success, your power, or your wealth.

It's about rewriting the rules for every woman who comes after you.

Now that you know, there's no unknowing.

The return begins here.

Begin again.

Begin Again

YOU'VE READ THE STORIES.
NOW IT'S TIME TO LIVE YOURS.

The characters in this book are fictional. The patterns behind them are not.

Their paths never crossed, yet their inner experiences mirror those of countless women I've advised over the past twenty years. Before I wrote this book, I spent two decades in the wealth management industry designing strategy for executives, business owners, generational wealth holders, and high-performing women navigating major financial and life transitions.

I've sat across from women making multi-million-dollar decisions while silently questioning themselves at the very moment they were being celebrated by others. What I learned was this: **wealth alone doesn't create clarity—self-trust does.**

The most meaningful shifts didn't come from refining strategy but from understanding *why* a decision was being made in the first place. Many of my clients were highly financially literate. What they lacked was the ability to interpret their choices through the lens of identity, conditioning, and personal authority. That's where financial psychology entered my work—not to change how women think about money, but to reveal how power, responsibility, and self-trust operate beneath every decision.

When appropriate, I integrated elements of human design—not to categorize, but to illuminate how someone is uniquely wired to make decisions. It was never about labels. It was about helping women build wealth from alignment rather than expectation.

From this work, four distinct expressions emerged:

- **Ava** reflects the woman whose achievement outpaced her sense of identity—driving her to pursue financial success as proof rather than expression.
- **Grace** mirrors the woman who has been entrusted with significant assets, yet pauses before stepping into authority with them—determined to steward them wisely.
- **Sarah** represents the woman who leads through service, often prioritizing others in her financial decisions at the cost of her own long-term clarity.
- **Elena** reflects the woman who accomplished what she set out to do and is now questioning whether her current financial success aligns with the life she actually wants next.

I've advised many versions of these women. Their industries and financial realities varied; what they shared was not a lack of capability, but a crossroads—a recognition that while expertise drives achievement, **self-trust is what makes their decisions honest.**

The women who moved through transition most powerfully tended to follow a natural internal progression:

Awareness → Language → Intention → Growth → Navigation.

This became the foundation of the **ALIGN Method**™ and the quiet architecture of this story.

If one of these characters stayed with you, you may be entering your own ALIGN progression. There is nothing to solve right now—only something to acknowledge.

Consider the following:

If you resonated with Ava:

Where have achievement and performance become interchangeable? What would it look like if success reflected who you are now—not who you were when you set that goal?

If you connected with Grace:

What have you already been entrusted with, and what would change if you claimed authority over it before feeling fully ready?

If Sarah felt familiar:

What are you still carrying because you can—not because you should? What might shift if honoring yourself became a responsible decision, not a luxurious one?

If Elena's story stayed with you:

What have you quietly outgrown—even if it still earns you respect? If freedom is no longer the finish line, what is?

You don't need to answer these questions right now.
You simply don't need to leave them behind.

If something stirred while reading, you are not alone. Increasingly, women are beginning to make decisions—from wealth to leadership—from internal clarity rather than expectation. Not by pushing harder, but by bringing more truth to what they choose next.

The book ends here. Your reinvention doesn't have to.

If you're ready to explore what this means for you, visit **ajbishopandrews.com/beginagain**.

Because wealth was never meant to stop at money. It was meant to begin with who you become.

The world will celebrate you when you're rich like her.
Your life will transform when you become rich like you.